ANCHORED
IN RESILIENCE

Overcoming Adversity through
Mental Health Awareness

* * * * * *

ANCHORED
IN RESILIENCE

AMAURY PONCIANO

Tampa, Florida

Anchored in Resilience: Overcoming Adversity through Mental Health Awareness

Published by Gatekeeper Press
7853 Gunn Hwy., Suite 209
Tampa, FL 33626
www.GatekeeperPress.com

The views expressed in this publication are those of the author and do not necessarily reflect the official policy or position of the Department of Defense or the U.S. government.

The public release clearance of this publication by the Department of Defense does not imply Department of Defense endorsement or factual accuracy of the material.

Library of Congress Control Number: 2023951483

ISBN (paperback): 9781662947216
eISBN: 9781662947223

Table of Contents

CHAPTER I

How do you write a book about you and your life without sounding full of yourself or exposing Amaury too much? Where is that sweet spot that enables you to tell your story without hurting others or yourself? My story is not special or uncommon, which makes it all that more shareable. My hope is to give you a glimpse into the life of a boy looking for love, a young man looking for answers, and a man wanting to inspire.

As you will learn through my story, counseling has become a major part of my life, just as much as my love for traveling. I bring that up because, in all my counseling sessions, we always discuss one thing: my upbringing. At first, I didn't grasp the significance, but meeting counselors made me realize that healing begins with understanding our wounds.

I was born in the Dominican Republic, a beautiful island shared with Haiti, in between Cuba and Puerto Rico. My parents were only married for a few years, with me being the only child out of that marriage. We were a middle-class family by Dominican standards, but that soon would change once my parents got divorced. When I was three, I stayed with my mother when my dad moved away to live with his mother and sisters. Living at your parents' house as an adult with a full family was extremely common in those days in the Dominican Republic. My mother was caring and devoted to me as her only son. We lived in the capital, Santo Domingo, but she always wanted to return to Mao, the providence where she was born and raised. She worked in a factory since she didn't have a degree, but she made decent money and did everything to support us. I remember that no matter how long her day was or how little she had financially, she would bring me a Hot Wheels car daily.

I can't recall much about those days with my mother, but I do recall her meeting someone and getting married when I was five. I can vividly remember not being happy about my mother loving someone else, and even more so, feeling hurt that she was pregnant, and that I was not going to be the only kid in the house.

I was an angry kid. Some of it was just having my mother's temper, and the other half was not receiving the love and affection that I badly craved. Now I understand how important affection and physical touch are to who I am. I am someone who loves hugging those I cherish, finding any reason to kiss my children, and holding hands while I explore a new city with the person I love. My physical touch tendencies have turned some people off or simply discouraged others since they saw my tendencies to get intimate instead of just a simple way to feel closer.

It is now 1985, and my mother is expecting a baby. I remember two episodes with my mother that will forever change my trajectory as a child. First, I grabbed a dinner knife and threatened to stab my mother's belly. To this day, I don't know, and truly don't want to know, how a five-year-old boy could embody that much hate and anger. My mother rightfully punished me by beating me with a belt, although I think it was a bit extreme to have me take a shower first to ensure I was dripping wet. That episode was the closest I would experience to what it must have felt like to be lashed as a slave.

The second episode was me telling my mother that I would be better living with my dad and that he loved me more than she did. I think back and ask myself, how can a five-year-old know that life is better with their dad? I can recall visiting my dad at his lavish apartment, with top-of-the-line electronics and brand-new furniture. There was food and snacks from the US, which is when I discovered Frosted Flakes cereal. Another luxury was that he never lost electricity, which is rare in the Dominican Republic due to frequent blackouts and a lack of generators for backup power. He also made very good money as the supervisor of the printing department and assistant to the plant superintendent at a cardboard box manufacturer.

I recall when my father was house-sitting an apartment for his drug-dealing cousin who lived in New York. She would only visit DR in the summer and sometimes during the Christmas holidays. She poured so much money into her home, it was like living in New York City, but with Dominican weather. For a time, my father also lived with another cousin in the Dominican Republic, who moved to the capital, Santo Domingo, to find a better life. She lived on the east of the island in a really poor town. She didn't have any children at the time, so she took care of me while my dad was at work. She cooked amazing food, she would help me with schoolwork, and she would even help me with my fashion sense, but she also would make me call her mom, and tell me that she cared about me more than my mother since she only had me and that my place was with her because she was just a better mother.

Now I want you to think about a child hearing that, and seeing a better life full of things one could only dream of. On top of that, receiving love and affirmation from a parent that a new brother could soon take away. All of that made me say hurtful things to my mother, which made me dislike her more; she couldn't give me Frosted Flakes or cook only for me.

One day out of the blue while having breakfast, I thought to myself that I could be living better. I could be having a better life, so I made my decision while having my breakfast, with no thoughts like I was making a decision of having hot chocolate instead of Frosted Flakes for breakfast. My mother was heartbroken when I asked to move in with my dad. She didn't even try to argue with me or even tell a young boy that he was wrong. She just started to cry. She angrily packed my belongings, called my dad around lunch time and demanded he pick me up and take me to his house, which was way before his workday ended. As the minutes passed, I started to think about my decision. I was scared and felt very lonely. She wouldn't talk to me; she just cried and smoked for hours. Although it was what I wanted, I was devastated to leave my mother, and I also realized how easily she let me go. My dad showed up around 2:00 p.m. and didn't say much to me or her, just grabbed my suitcases and got me in his car. I remember looking back as the car drove away and she was not there; she couldn't even come outside because she was so angry, sad, and disappointed.

A new life began for me, living with my father and his cousin; we will call her "Juanita" for the purpose of the story. I was happy to be in a better school, with fancier clothes, eating food I never had access to before, and being shown love by my father and his family. My father was very calm and soft-spoken; he would be loving in his own way by teaching me how to play dominoes or doing math problems, which would get more complex as I solved them. As the months went on, I slowly realized that I was seeing my mother less and less, while Juanita was continuing to pressure me to call her mom. So much so, that she would beat me if I didn't. I don't know if it was because she wanted a child so badly or just a way to control, but it broke me. I have been able to forgive and, in some cases, forget about the things that happened during that time, but one memory will stay with me forever. My mother, tired of not being able to talk to me over the phone or see me, came to my dad's apartment and demanded to see me. My dad's cousin opened the door but refused to allow my mom inside or let me go to her. I could see my mom's face full of agony and despair, yet I was frozen, I couldn't move! I just watched, frozen in my steps, as the door slammed in her face.

I know some may ask why my mother didn't do more. I asked myself the same question as I got older, but thankfully I was able to have that conversation with her almost thirty years after that hurtful day. She later opened up about her financial struggles. My dad not only had a high-paying job but also the backing of his drug-dealing cousin, who spared no expense to make her family happy, which included me living with them. The Dominican Republic justice system favors those who have money, so my mother knew that fighting for custody would have been money down the drain for someone who already didn't have much.

Time passed, and I became tired of my father's lack of affection and Juanita's manipulation. By this time, I was eight, and my mother was getting ready to move to the US with her new husband and my twin brothers. She finally found love again and started dating an old high school sweetheart. They got married and my youngest brother, Lazaro, came along. Her new husband was living in the US, so after the marriage ceremony, he left to continue to work in New York while my mother stayed with my grandparents in the small town where they're from, Mao. My mother had twins, and, unfortunately, during the pregnancy she was stressed and depressed, which resulted in her smoking habits. This had a major effect on one of my baby brothers. He was born with an oversized lung, which was never diagnosed, and eight months after he was born, his little body couldn't take it. He died the day of my grandma's birthday, and a day before my mother's birthday. His death will always haunt my mother. She will never forgive herself for my brother being born with an oversized lung due to her smoking. I was so young that I remember crying because I saw others crying, not necessarily because I felt like crying. I knew I was sad, but I really didn't know my brothers.

Since my parents were divorced, the only way my mother could submit for my visa was with my father's permission. He would not consent, for a reason I would discover years later. He was afraid I would get into drugs, with my mother moving to New Jersey, and that I would be another Dominican kid getting into trouble in NYC. All that is fair if you ask me, but that was not the message conveyed to me by him and his cousin. Months after my mother left for the US, I started asking why I didn't go with her, and their answer would rock my eight-year-old mind forever... They said that she left me. They didn't tell me the truth about my father refusing to sign the papers, but instead that my mother made the choice to move to another country with my brothers and her husband and didn't want to take me. Do you know what that does to a child? The level of pain and disbelief that crosses his mind, his heart, and his soul. I was broken and angry. Because of the hurt and confusion, I asked my parents if I could move to my aunt Sonia's house. She was my godmother, and the one that took me to the airport to say goodbye to my mother, and the closest family member I had left.

My father approved, and I started living with my aunt, uncle, and two cousins. My aunt was loving and caring; she truly loved me because she believed my mother being pregnant with me and me becoming her godson was what helped her body prepare to get pregnant after over five years of trying. She was so focused on her job, her family, and being a wife and mother. My being there was unfair to her, but at that time I desperately needed an adult who would put me first, to be taken care of, and most of all, loved. I was her nephew and godson, but her children were the priority, and rightfully so. She would give them the bigger piece of chicken, and they would be celebrated more for their success in school, yet I still felt loved and taken care of. For the first time, I felt important to an adult. She displayed love by talking to me about her day while I was helping her with the dishes. It's funny because, in adult relationships, I have always told my significant other that doing dishes is my thing. It brings me a level of comfort and peace, and takes me back to my childhood since those conversations with my aunt were not the only ones I encountered while doing the dishes.

I did well in school, contributed to the household, and even helped at the car wash my aunt and uncle owned. The place was amazing! You would drop your car in one of the slots and wait for it at a table where you could order drinks and food—Dominicans don't believe in DUIs. Some evenings the parking lot and car wash would be closed and there would be live music. There was lots of merengue, bachata, and salsa while the kids bussed tables for tips. I won't lie, those were some of the best moments of my life. I remember my mother visiting from New York in the summer and hanging out with us, drinking, eating, and dancing with me. I recall my father coming to see me at the car wash and having me in his lap while playing dominoes and drinking. It would be for a short time, but it was so meaningful.

Unfortunately, with time, the car wash started to fail, and that brought stress to my aunt and uncle, spilling over to the kids. They would ask me why my parents didn't send more money, take me for the summer, or take me back with them. I know now those things were said out of anger, but to an abandoned ten-year-old, the words were like sharp knives digging into my skin. One summer, everything came to a head. My grandmother on my mom's side had already passed away, and now my grandfather was dying. I don't believe in love at first sight, or dying from a broken heart, but I do know my grandad's health significantly deteriorated within a year of losing my grandmother. Not having my grandma around just didn't make sense to him, and he'd rather die than live life without her.

While on his deathbed, my grandad asked my father why he didn't sign my US citizenship paperwork and wanted to know why he was taking away the opportunity for me to have a better life. My dad always had a huge amount of respect for my grandad and loved him very much. This was 1991, and my grandfather's passing pushed my dad to finally sign the documents. I was so happy, but deep down I was hurt. It was a confusing moment for a child. I felt abandoned because my mother left me three years before that.

During that time, there were also a lot of changes with where I would live, because of my aunt and uncle's deteriorating financial circumstances. That summer it was decided that I was going to live with a different aunt. My aunt Fatima was from my mother's side, she kept a more structured household, was firmer, and was basically my mother's twin from looks to temper. Her husband was just as strict and wanted their kids and me to be in Catholic schools. Because incomes in the Dominican Republic are near the poverty level, Catholic schools were funded by donations and payments from families with children enrolled.

I was required to get high grades, complete chores, and be obedient. I learned so much from my aunt and two female cousins. I would be the only male in the house who would do chores, which meant I'd hear about work and marriage from my aunt, boy gossip and work from my twenty-year-old cousin, and mostly about school from my sixteen-year-old cousin. I will admit, I heard and was asked for advice on things an eleven-year-old shouldn't have knowledge of, much less be advising. I was doing what I loved: getting to be in adult conversations, receiving words of encouragement, affirmation about soon seeing my mother, and being encouraged for my achievements in school. Those words are still with me today, and it allowed me to focus even at a young age because I saw that focus in my sixteen-year old cousin. It made me want to get the best grades I could, and the fact that our school would give scholarships to the best student in each grade was an even bigger motivator. I didn't want to be a burden to my aunt and uncle, and if I could get the next school year for free plus uniforms and school supplies, then I was going to try my hardest.

The way the school was broken down was simple—it was an all-male Catholic school, with the girls across the street. Each grade had four to five classes, so there were five fifth-grade classes, with about 160 students total. I wanted so badly to be loved by my aunt, uncle, and parents that I applied all my energy to school. I was selected student of the year for my fifth, sixth, and seventh grade classes, which meant tuition was free. It helped that I was bad at sports, especially baseball. Playing baseball is something that every Dominican kid does from the tender age of two. It is an escape from poverty and a ticket to a better life. I was disappointed I was not able to give my family that opportunity.

Although I was disappointed, I didn't let it affect me too much. I just focused on my studies and the little bit of athleticism I had, which was enough to enjoy sports games and be competitive. I was still being compared with my cousin, who was a competitive baseball player, but not so much of a student. Like true teenagers, he would find every opportunity to remind me of how bad I was at baseball, and I would remind him how much better I was in school.

Over time, just like at my other aunt's house, things with money started to become an issue, and again I was subjected to ugly comments about my parents not providing enough to cover my room and board, and that I was not doing enough in the house. I must admit that looking back, I wish my parents had done more. There's no way that two different households could be lying about the lack of funds my parents provided. Children are expensive, especially if you are already buying food, clothing, and items for your own family. It is another mouth to feed, another person consuming electricity and adding to the laundry. I don't blame my family for being frustrated. I just wish that frustration was expressed to my parents instead of me.

During my high school years, I was super skinny and unathletic, so I was shy and very insecure. I only had memories of my time in the Dominican Republic, where I was made fun of because of my dimples, my grey hair, and even my dark skin. My self-esteem was at an all-time low.

I want to share about the culture in the Dominican Republic. I want to start by saying that I love my island, I love my culture, our food, our music, and how resilient our people are. I'm so proud to come from that beautiful island. All that said, it is important to talk about how my people hate their skin if they're not light-skinned or white. From an early age, you are told things like "don't stay out in the sun too much, because you will get dark," "don't drink coffee, because it will make you black," or "have babies with someone white so you refine the race." All those things I heard from people who I know are good people and would never consider themselves racist. It is so ingrained in our minds that comments like that are seen as just jokes or ways to keep children from doing bad things. I was around it so much, and those comments came from white and black Dominicans.

CHAPTER II

The years passed, and the visa process was happening in the background. The visa process can be very long, time-consuming, and costly. You have to show bank statements, taxes from prior years, proof of employment, and fill out tons of paperwork. The day finally came when I got to do my citizenship interview. I remember my mother reminding me of important dates like her birthday, my brother's birthday, and her ex-husband's name since he was the one who got her the visa, so they would ask about him. She reminded me of details about what my father did for a living and the reasons why I was coming to the US. I remember my mom telling me how important this interview was, and how my answers could be the difference between me getting the visa or having to wait five years before I apply again. The interview was intense, very detailed, and had a lot of questions for a thirteen-year-old, but I did well enough to get my visa! I was so happy to finally move to the US and live with my mother.

I had to wait three months. Finally, a week after my fourteenth birthday, I was going to fly for the very first time in my life and be with my mother. I knew life would be different since she was remarried, and my brother was eight and didn't speak Spanish well. My mother purchased a direct flight from Santo Domingo to John F. Kennedy Airport. She also sent me a yellow sweater since it would be the first time that I was going to experience temperatures under fifty degrees. I can't remember how the flight was, but I remember how nervous I was carrying a big folder full of paperwork, knowing that I was going to be stopped by immigration once I landed in New York.

Finally, I landed, and I felt the cold fall air for the first time. I pulled on my yellow sweater. As I approached the immigration agent, I felt my heart wanting to jump out of my little chest, my dry mouth, and my hands shake. The agent didn't speak Spanish, and I didn't speak English, so he looked a bit annoyed, but since I was a child, he went easy on me. He asked for a translator, asked a few questions, and provided me with my temporary green card. A lady who spoke Spanish helped me navigate to baggage claim, and as I emerged, I saw my mother's big smile. She was so happy to see me and gave me the second biggest hug she had ever given me.

My life completely changed at that moment; a new world was about to unfold, and to be honest, I was not ready. We lived in Union City, New Jersey, which was a family-oriented community full of Hispanics. There were signs in Spanish all around the city, including in Chinese restaurants, which also had Hispanic food like fried plantains, fried salami, and more. It was so overwhelming, yet super exciting about what the US had to offer. After a week of getting to know the city, applying for my Social Security number, and just learning how life would be, I was enrolled in school.

My mother would allow me to walk around the neighborhood so I could get used to the streets since I would have to walk to and from school. The main streets had names; my street was Summit Ave., and the perpendicular streets were numbered. Our apartment was located between Eleventh and Twelfth street on Summit Ave. My mother had a small bodega on Twelfth street, which helped me get more acquainted with my surroundings by getting to know the community. Helping her bag the customers' products and having conversations with them was, in a way, a safe place. They spoke Spanish like me and had a lot of mannerisms you would see in the Dominican Republic.

Edison Middle School was only ten blocks from my house, so I would walk there with my little brother Lazaro. I was in a program called English as a Second Language, or ESL, so I could learn English. I was blessed with three teachers who were super-proud Latin Americans. They wanted all of us to be successful, so they pushed and mentored us about how to navigate life in the US as immigrants, how to work hard in school so we didn't have to work in factories like our parents, and how to return the favor to our parents in the future was the biggest accomplishment possible. Eighth grade was fun. I was reading books faster than others just because I didn't feel challenged enough compared to my classes in the Dominican Republic. I was still super skinny and dressed poorly. I had jeans and shirts from Walmart or even hand-me-downs. My shoes were new but not anything in style and from Payless, yet I started to get the interest of the ladies like I never did back home. This would become another struggle in my life; it was like obtaining fame. I was in no way prepared or mentally mature enough for the attention I received from women. I had no clue how to handle it, but I navigated it to the best of my ability yet hurt people along the way.

For example, I was asked by six girls to be their Valentine. One asked me during lunch. She came to my table and asked me what I was doing the night of Valentine's Day, and was I going to the party? I said nothing. Then she asked, "Do you want to go with me?" I didn't know it was an invitation to the dance or what it meant. Another simply passed me a small piece of paper that said "Valentine dance with me, yes or no." And the others just simply asked me after my English teacher asked if I had a date, and I shook my head no. So she asked, "Would anybody like to go to the dance with Amaury?" and three or four raised their hands, but I was so shy that I didn't commit to anyone or give any Valentines out. The school was going well, like it has most of my life, but home was a different story. The home was full of arguments and pain. I was angry that my brother already spoke fluent English and got to be around my mother all this time. I was angry that she married someone else, and I was angry that she left me. I believe it is important to give context to my mother being married again. What I'm about to tell you might sound like it is from a movie or a novella, as we say in Latin America, but no, it is something real that happened to my mother, and to this day I still feel her pain.

My mother has had a very rough life, full of lies, pain, and challenges. She had to deal with things a child shouldn't have to, things that would scar her for life. I won't go into details about those things in her childhood because that's her story, and I don't want to open old wounds. I can start by telling you that because of those wounds she would always be guarded, felt unloved, and overall unsafe. She married my dad a few years before I was born, and quickly discovered that he was more worried about taking care of his parents and siblings than his wife and future child.

Things came to a head when my grandfather hit my mother with a pan in the nose, not necessarily on purpose, since he just threw the pan in her direction without looking, but it did break her nose. To make things worse, neither my grandfather nor my dad apologized. That, along with other issues they had as a couple, made my mother decide to get divorced. She struggled on her own as a single mother, both financially and emotionally, yet she continued to fight and do her best for me and my brothers.

Once she remarried after my father, she had to endure more suffering and pain. She applied for a Visa to come to the US. Months passed by, and she was waiting for her paperwork to be processed so she and my brother could get a visa to come to the US to live with her husband. Her journey to the US was difficult. She ended up getting a visa and traveled to New York with my baby brother. Her husband picked her up and took her to a friend's house to stay since the drive to his house would be long. He wanted to take a break before they continued to drive. Once they arrived at the friend's house, he told my mother: "Here is

$200; I am going to get some milk and food for the house." My mother waited and waited, and he never came back. I can't even fathom how she felt in this new country, with a new language, and an infant in a stranger's house. She would tell me later about her agony and stress knowing she had to care for my brother with no roof over their heads, no job, and no support system.

As time would show me, my mother was the epitome of resilience, a woman driven by the desire to do anything and everything for her children. She started making phone calls and finding a way to get somewhere within the US where she could take my brother Lazaro. Thankfully, she had a brother who lived in Queens, New York, and he was graceful enough to open his door to her.

She then had to make the tough decision to send my brother back to the Dominican Republic so he could live with my grandparents while she established herself. My mother soon found a job at a factory in Queens. She had to develop skills that she never studied or was trained for; her job required her to be standing for over seven hours while picking up and moving large painting frames. Her role was to distress art frames to look antique. She would use tools like mosquito spray, spider web spray, and small hammers to make "time dents." She became really good at it rather quickly and was able to get pay raises every six months for two years straight.

During that time, she had to struggle living with my uncle. Her room was a small corner in the living room covered by curtains. There was no privacy, no space, and a very crowded house. A little over a year after being in the US, she met a man and they started dating. Funny enough, it was the son of the stranger she was dropped off with when arriving in the country. He had previously been a drug dealer and in gangs in New York City, but turned his life around about ten years before they met. He made her feel safe, helped her get a place on her own, and encouraged her to find a way to be with her children again.

Her first decision once she was in her own place was to get my brother back. She wasn't able to bring me to the US at that time because my father had not signed the visa papers. My brother joined her and her soon-to-be husband. They developed a good bond as a family, and my brother had that father he never had.

Things with my mother and her husband would change, but that's later on. In 1994, now I was part of the family. My mother still worked in the factory, making good money for factory work, and her husband was a retailer, who through under-the-table deals was able to resell merchandise to bodegas, which is Spanish for "little market." He sold things like laundry detergent, sodas, and many other things that could make a profit. After a few years of making good profits and having a set route, he decided with my mother to open their own bodega. Unfortunately, the location was not the best since it wasn't a high-foot-traffic area, and was not close to any schools, parks, or anything that would bring a lot of people. They continued to pour money into it, getting loans and even making the family go without to make it work. Thankfully, another bodega at another location, a much better location, with two schools within five blocks, and two huge parks, had been put up for sale at a good price due to the sudden death of the owner. My mother and her husband were able to sell the current bodega and clear the debts while also buying the new one in Jersey City, New Jersey.

While all this was happening, we were living at the poverty level. I would honestly say we were living maybe a level above the poverty level in the Dominican Republic. Like in most relationships, the issues with money brought a lot of stress and fighting between my mother and her husband. He started drinking again and being verbally abusive. At the same time, I was a fourteen-year-old bitter and rebellious teenager, incredibly angry about my mother leaving me and about my brother knowing English because he was with my mother for a long period of time. I would be defiant at every opportunity. My mother would ask me to do something, and my response was always, "I don't know or want to do that because you didn't teach me any of that, since you left me." This was constant for over a year. Lots of arguments, lots of tears, and lots of accusations. I was angry, depressed, and feeling very alone in a house where I still didn't feel loved. Right before Christmas of 1995, my mother had had enough of the way I was treating her and how I was accusing her of leaving. We had one phone line at the house but two phones, one in the kitchen and another in my mother's room. Me and my mother got into another heated argument, and while she was crying, she said, "I'm going to call your father; I just want you to listen on the other phone." She did, and asked him point blank, "Why did you lie to Amaury and say that I left him, when in reality you didn't want to sign the papers to get him his visa?" My father didn't have anything to say, and while crying, I spoke up and asked him if that was true, meaning that all this time he was just lying to me. He stayed silent and didn't answer, so that was my answer.

At that moment, my mother became my sun, my world, and my best friend. Our relationship was stronger and growing, but her relationship with her husband was getting worse. He was becoming more abusive with her, me, and even more with my younger brother. I hated it. As the older brother, I wanted to fight him. I wanted to protect my mother and my baby brother. One day he came home drunk, and he was saying some awful things to my mother, including "I need to pee, open your mouth so I can pee in it." I grabbed a bat, and I wanted to hit him. Thankfully, my mother stopped me, because I would have been in jail for a very long time. From that point forward, I had no respect for him. I was upset with my mother for not leaving him, for putting us through that, and most of all, for keeping my brother in an environment with so much verbal abuse.

Once I was in high school, I enjoyed the success I had in my classes and felt very proud that after only three years in the US, I was in all English classes. I had nice clothes, and for the first time in my life, I was getting new clothes every week. That doesn't mean much to others, but for me it was so amazing because I grew up with nothing, or clothing that had been used by two or three people before it got to me. I was popular in school, and I was getting the girls' attention, which for a fifteen- or sixteen-year-old was heaven.

I was one of the leaders in my friend group, which built my confidence to talk to women and be more proactive. I met a lot of amazing people in high school, from other students to teachers. But without a doubt, the most important person I met was my best friend, Donny. He was the one person who understood my anger by just letting me get it out and move forward. He would push me to get out of my comfort zone without being pushy or mean. I learned so much about myself just by hanging out with him and his family. They demonstrated what a functional family looked like, and their home was full of love, even if they were struggling since his mother was a single mom. I would visit his house, and we would talk about our day and the things we learned and saw in school. His mom would talk about work, and she would always be positive about life and positive about the things we would complain about. She was realistic, not just simply saying things to be positive, but saying things that would encourage and uplift us.

I had a really big complex about my skin color and my appearance, as I said before, so for years, I didn't want to be called Black, and I would even correct people that I was Dominican, not Black. I didn't like to be associated with what I believed was another race. I would argue with other kids while in school and even years into my enlistment in the Navy. I would have never admitted to others, but the reality was that I didn't want to be associated with African Americans. It's not that I disliked them, or that I thought I was better. In my eyes, we were just different. I was a Dominican who spoke differently, dressed differently, and danced and cooked differently. Thankfully, a few things happened in my life that made me understand that I was a Black Dominican and that I needed to be proud of that.

It is 1998 and I am a junior now. I was in the top ten of my class and my English was getting better each day. I also worked on Saturdays with my mom's husband, helping pick up and deliver the products he would resell to bodegas at a marked down price, which was cheaper than the actual supplier. So, for example, if a bottle of Tide detergent would cost $5.60 in the bodega, then usually the Tide company would sell it to the bodega for $5.00, which meant a $0.60 profit. Here is where my mom's husband would come into play. He would either have us cut coupons or buy in bulk, which meant that each Tide detergent would cost him anywhere from $2.99 to $3.99, then he would sell it to the bodega for $4.00 or $4.50, which meant that it was cheaper than the manufacturer and meant bigger profits. He did that with at least thirty to forty products, and I helped him pick up, transfer, and deliver the products for quick cash. Those Saturdays we would get up at 5:00 a.m., which was torture for a young teenager. We would finish at 8:00 p.m. or later, but the long day was worth it. It was good pay for a day's work since sometimes he would pay me between $80 to $120.

I also did chores in the house, like doing the dishes (I still loved doing them), sweeping, taking out the trash and, most importantly, staying at home with my brother from the time we left school until my mother got home from work so she didn't have to pay for an after-school program. Because of that, my mom used to give me $25 to $50 weekly. I spent all that money on clothes and shoes that I didn't need. Having nice clothes and a nice haircut every two weeks gave me a sense of security about my image that was only superficial, but it was what I needed at the time. It was a small piece of happiness since I was uneasy about how my mother's husband treated her and my brother, as well as being confused about what would be my next step in life. I was not sure about college, between not having the financial resources and not really wanting to go to school for another four years; my desire to go to college was diminishing each day.

My mom's husband was in the Army for a few years, so he started talking about the military and how it could provide discipline and an opportunity to be successful. I was not sure but was also desperate for certainty in my future, and I wanted to repay my mother for all of her sacrifices. So I went to a recruiting office in Jersey City, New Jersey. It was one of those offices that had a big hallway with multiple doors. Behind each door, there were recruiters, each from a different branch of the military. I started talking to an Army recruiter, and he was super excited that I wanted to join, so he took me to the Military Entrance Processing Station (MEPS) in Brooklyn so I could take my Armed Services Vocational Aptitude Battery (ASVAB), which was the test utilized to predict and measure the success in a career field of an individual who wanted to join the military. My recruiter did not express how important this exam was to the selection of a career field, just simply that I needed to pass. He picked me up at 4:00 a.m. and we drove for an hour. We had a quick breakfast and then I took a test that felt like it lasted six or seven hours, but it was only four. I received my scores, and overall, they were decent. The test was divided into nine parts, from general science to mathematics to automotive and mechanical knowledge. My English was still very underdeveloped; it was only my second year of all English classes. This was evident in my test scores, but my math was super high, which would help later. A few weeks later, I sat down with a recruiter to talk about my score and what jobs I could apply for in the Army. I really wanted to do something with computers and networks. I didn't know much about either, but I wanted to learn. The recruiter only offered infantry; no matter what I said, his answer was infantry.

I left upset and disappointed. I went to my best friend's house to talk to him about what happened and how I felt. He asked me if I had talked to the Navy recruiter and said that he was going into the Navy, and the recruiter could probably help me too. The next day, I was back in the recruiting office. I explained my situation to the Navy recruiter, and he asked how I did on the ASVAB. I said I scored a fifty-five, and he said that was decent. I told him if he got my paperwork from the Army recruiter, I would join the Navy. He got up and came back about fifteen minutes later with my record. I could hear the Army recruiter cursing me out for wasting his time, but as I later learned, the Navy was the right path for me.

The Navy recruiter didn't promise me a specific job field but told me all the things the Navy had to offer—traveling around the world, money for college, health care benefits, job security, and technical skills. I was excited because on the wall behind his desk he had over fifty pictures of places he had traveled while in the Navy, and in at least thirty of them he was surrounded by beautiful women. That sparked the interest of a seventeen-year-old. In his photos, I also saw a Chief Petty Officer wearing a long-sleeved, dark blue uniform with a tie. It was fully dark blue, and all the ribbons and warfare devices were in different colors, which made them pop even more against the contrast of the dark blue.

Right after my eighteenth birthday, the recruiter took me to the MEPS station again. This time, they would complete my physical examination and I'd be assigned a career field. The amount of checks they do on your body is crazy, from flexibility, balance, eye exams, and much more. After drug tests, blood work, and hours and hours of testing, I finally sat down to sign my Navy contract. This is also where you select a career field. At first, they were talking about a few administrative jobs, then logistics supply jobs, but I wouldn't break from my determination to get a job in the computer science field. Finally, he said that he could offer me a computer science job, but that my English scores were low, and I would need a waiver. He said that due to my high math scores, I would be able to get a waiver. Sure enough, the waiver was approved, and I joined the Navy as a radioman or RM. Radiomen in the Navy are personnel who specialize in communications and network technology. I left so happy, and my recruiter was waiting for me in the parking lot. He had warned me not to take just any job or apprenticeship program since I had a good score on the ASVAB. I told him I picked RM, and he smiled and said, "Awesome, I'm an RM2." I looked at him with a face of both confusion and anger and asked why he didn't advise me to pick RM if he knew that was the career field I wanted. He responded he wanted me to pick my own future, and that he was there to get me in the Navy, not make choices for my career.

With that taken care of, I focused on my senior year. The pressure of going to college was gone, and the hormones of a teenage boy were kicking in hard. Up to that point, I was very shy and insecure around women, but between hanging with my best friends and having money in my pockets as well as having nice clothes, shoes, and colognes, my confidence was getting a lot higher. It was mostly superficial confidence, but confidence nonetheless. I skipped classes to hang out with my friends and girls, went to parties Friday and Saturday nights, and messed around with older girls.

The summer between my junior and senior year, I was vacationing in the Dominican Republic, which was the tradition since I came to the US. It was a way for me to see my dad, my cousins, aunts, and uncles, plus a break for my mother since she would send me and my brother there for the entire summer. In the summer of 1998, I met a girl in my dad's neighborhood; she was so beautiful. Long black hair, light caramel skin, hazel eyes, and the body of a woman! Curvy, yet with a super small waist, and she was three years older than me and even had a kid already. She was living in New York City and was spending the summer in DR, like me. We met at a house party and hit it off right away. She was into me even though guys way older than me were trying to talk to her; she only paid attention to me. It was such a high; not only that a beautiful woman was paying attention to a seventeen-year-old, but she was also ignoring twenty-four- and twenty-five-year-old men for me. As we talked and spent more time together, it was clear that she wanted to have sex with me, but until that point, I had only gone as far as oral sex with a woman. We also didn't have a place to have sex. She was staying with her family, and I was as well. I didn't have enough money to pay for a hotel, and I was not going to ask her to get one. I was getting worried that she would get tired of the little boy, and so I looked for other ideas. Fortunately, my cousin had a brilliant idea. He said his mom went to work at eight in the morning, and he was usually home on his own until she returned at five. He told me to come by around nine with her, and we could have the house.

We showed up at nine and he left, locked the main door, and we had the house to ourselves. She had to be back by noon, and I knew I only had a few hours before my family would start asking where I was. As you might have expected, the first sexual encounter was super basic and fast. I think I took longer undressing her and kissing her than I did having sex. But I was not discouraged; we laid down and kissed and talked, and did it again and again. It was getting closer to noon, so we showered and thought that we would head out, but it was then that we discovered that the main door only unlocked with a key, which my cousin took with him. I couldn't remember where he was going to be and I only knew the phone number of two places. This was back before cell phones. We started screaming and finally got the attention of a little kid passing by. I gave him $5 and a promise of another $10 if he found my cousin. After about forty-five minutes, the kid found my cousin and he opened the door.

Talk about a morning full of excitement. Like most good things in life, once I had the taste of having sex, I was hooked. I wanted to keep finding places to see her and enjoy her. It only happened a couple of times more and she had to return to New York City. We promised that we would see each other in the US and be together, and we actually tried for a few months after the summer ended. I took the train to the Bronx and visited her. We went out to eat, and I paid for hotels so we could be alone, but little by little she started to pull away. I really think that she finally realized she was dealing with a boy. I couldn't take her out to clubs, since I was under twenty-one, couldn't stay the night because I had a curfew, and couldn't help her with the bills for her and her kid. Of course, all those observations have only become clear as I've gotten older and have reflected on my past. At the time it was happening, I couldn't understand why, and I was heartbroken. My mom didn't like her, simply because she was older and had a child, but she could see how much I cared about her. She tried to console me and told me that things would get better, and that life moves on.

I will say that I learned a lot in those five months about myself and what I enjoyed sexually. I would still learn a lot more, but it was my first experience with my body and, most importantly, the body of a woman.

After the breakup, I was a Don Juan or Casanova if you will, or at least I thought so. My confidence was on another level, and I was able to talk to any girl I liked. I was not afraid of rejection, and I was getting more comfortable around women. I had sex with three other girls my senior year, all of them at someone else's house or their house. My mom had a strict rule that she didn't want me having sex in her house. She would actually say, "If anybody is fucking in this house, it's me." She wasn't naive enough to think that a seventeen-, eighteen-year-old boy was not going to want to have sex; so every month, she gave me $50 extra from my allowance so I could use it for a hotel room. She also got me condoms. It sounds wild, but she just wanted me to be safe and not try to hide the fact that I was sexually active.

One day, I met Stephanie at the park down the street from my home. She was the closest thing to my dream woman at the time, Pamela Anderson. She was tall, blonde, and had big breasts. We started seeing each other, but nothing serious; we just watched movies and had sex. Stephanie's parents had money. Her dad was a surgeon, and her mom was a lawyer. They lived a few blocks away from my house, but it was two different worlds. One day, her family was going to Macy's on thirty-fourth Avenue in New York. Stephanie insisted that I join, and since her parents spoiled her, they said yes. I remember I saw an all-black Avirex jacket, one that I had seen in a music video. I tried it on, and it looked great on me, but I looked at the price and it cost over $400. This was in 1998, so think about how expensive that would be today. Probably in the range of $900 to $1500. Her mother saw me try it on and said to get it, which right away I said no. This is because I knew my mother would think I stole it and would beat me until the next day. So we returned to their house a few hours later, and after having sex with Stephanie, I was walking out of the house when the mom approached me and said, "Here, this is for you." I couldn't believe it; it was the jacket!! In a fancy garment bag and everything. I was so happy and so excited that I forgot about how my mother would react.

I got home and put the jacket in my closet. My mom didn't see it or even say anything for days. In my head, I was going to wait a few weeks so she thought that I had saved the money from working and my allowance. Well, I was very wrong. My mother woke me up Saturday morning in a panic and super upset. She kept asking where I got the jacket, and I kept thinking, "How did you find it?" I got brave since I didn't want to lose the jacket, and asked how she found it today. She said, "This is my house, and every Saturday I go through every closet and drawer to see what's in my house, and I know this jacket was not here last week." I tried to make her believe that I got it with the money I earned, but she had already seen the other things I had gotten through the week, and the math was not adding up. Finally, I told her who got it for me, and she got even more upset. To her, I was taking charity from someone rich, and she was too proud to be accepting gifts. Or she was thinking that I was sleeping with a grown woman, because as she put it, "No woman who is not getting some dick would buy something that expensive, let alone for a boy." I was so upset, but I had to take the jacket back. The mom tried to tell me that she could talk to my mother and explain. I told her that one, my mother didn't speak English so that would be difficult, and two, that she didn't trust her already.

I kept talking to other girls since Stephanie and I weren't serious, but I always came back to her because she was open to a lot of things sexually and her house was super nice. One day, all would change. She told me to come over around five on a Saturday, and her parents would be gone for the weekend with her little sister. I was so eager to see her and have sex, so I was there at 4:58! To my surprise, her mother opened the door, wearing only a robe. I didn't think much of it and asked about her daughter. She said that she was still at her girlfriend's house but would be home soon. I asked if I could wait in the living room, and she said of course. As I sat there, I remembered that Stephanie used to love going to her friend's house to get high. So I said to myself, give it fifteen more minutes before you go. As I waited, her mom came and started picking up the toys the little sister had left in the living room, and some were right in front of the TV. When she bent down, her robe rode up and I saw that she wasn't wearing panties. As any eighteen-year-old would, I got hard and I couldn't stop looking. She looked back and smiled. She asked if I was okay, and I said yes, but we both could see that I was hard as a rock. Well, I won't say it was like the movies, where it was all smooth and I had sex with her. I mean I did, but it was super fast and the little bit I knew back then was all gone because I was too excited that I was sleeping with a woman. In the next three months, I had sex with her more than with her daughter, but I was sleeping with both. One day, when I called, her dad said to me that I had to leave because he was sending his daughter to a rehab center and he knew about me and his wife. He said it was ok, but no more. I was too scared to even call back.

Back at school, my senior year was moving along. I asked my freshman-year girlfriend to go to the prom with me, and she said yes. I made her promise as we were breaking up that she would go with me no matter who we had in our lives at the time of the prom. I look back and think about the balls I had to demand that she go with me after she broke up with me because I cheated. I also went places with my friends, like the lake, parks in other cities, and games for the basketball and volleyball teams. I was more involved with life; home life was not as bad as before, but my mother's husband was still there so I was not completely happy at home.

My group of friends wanted to have a memorable prom, so we started saving money and I was put in charge of booking everything. I had to find a place for the tuxedos, book the limo, find the after-party location, and even look for a house at the shore for the weekend. The first thing that fell off was getting a house on the shore; it was too much money and my mother was not going to let me spend a weekend away with my friends. Booking the limo was an adventure since we wanted something very extravagant, yet didn't have the money for it. We settled on a nice all-black limo that we would rent for eight hours, with snacks and drinks. Next, to find a place that rented tuxedos. We all had different styles, and I found a perfect place that was not too expensive. It was very nice and had a very simple return policy, which was important for irresponsible kids.

As each item was checked off the list, other events occurred. I ran across town and hid in different houses during the days I skipped school, and went to clubs with fake IDs, even if I had to be back at my house by eleven for curfew. My grades were nothing like in the first three years, and my class ranking dropped from the top 20 to the top 100, but I didn't care because I was not going to college. I didn't study for the SATs. I did enough to pass, but nothing special. I didn't get a driver's license, since one of our friends had a car and public transportation was very reliable in my hometown.

Finally, it was time for prom. Everything ran smoothly, and we got picked up on time by the limo. We all had our flowers for our dates, and we were able to get the driver to drive us around New York City after the prom for food and, hopefully, drinks. None of us got lucky with the ladies but that was ok; we danced all night and made memories. Like the time we lost a ribbon because a lady would ask us for one for the trade of a kiss, or get our dinner tab paid for because we were in the military. Those are some of the memories that we look back on today and smile. About three weeks later, we had a high school graduation and our class graduation party. My mother hated tattoos but allowed me to get one as my graduation gift; as usual, she paid for it even after arguing that she wouldn't. The tattoo was a cross with the yin-yang sign and the sun in the background. For the graduation party, they opened the indoor pool for the senior class and had food and a DJ from six until midnight. It was another evening that was full of memorable moments, laughs, and the understanding that it might be the last time we all saw each other.

I spoke with my Navy recruiter again, and he said that I would be leaving for boot camp on the first of August 1999. This was just six weeks after graduating. I was super nervous, so I asked my mother if she could send us to DR for the summer again, even if only for four weeks. She agreed and said that she wanted me to have a great time with my family in DR and then spend a week with her before leaving for boot camp.

I knew my best friend was going to boot camp, like me, but everyone else had different plans. Some wanted to go to school, and others already had jobs that, although didn't look like a long-term career, at that moment provided a good income. So we said our goodbyes, and the next day I headed to DR with my little brother. It was only thirty days, but I had a blast. I went out with my cousins to discos, went to the beach, went sightseeing at places that I had never seen in my country, and visited family that I had not seen in years.

Everything was going beautifully until my father took me to see his cousin Juanita, the lady who had forced me to call her mom. The lady who hung up on my mother or wouldn't let her see me. I was so angry and disappointed at my father and ready to be as rude as I could be. I remember pulling up to the house and her waiting for us with a huge smile, ready to hug me. I got out of the car and hardly moved; she came to me and hugged me but I didn't hug her. I knew the real story now, so not only was I cold to her and didn't say anything, but I also got into it with my father to have the balls to think that it would be appropriate. I sat there for a couple of hours hardly saying anything, but they both knew that I was not happy and that things would never be the same with me and her. Thankfully, that was the only negative moment of that trip. I had so many family members wish me well and tell me how proud they were of me for joining the military.

My brother and I returned to New Jersey, and my mother took a few days off just to do things with us and especially with me. Things were going a lot better with her and her husband, at least on the surface. They decided they wanted to move back to the DR, so they bought land and started building their dream house. They also put money into an account that would help set up the business they had in mind, which was buying goods wholesale and reselling to bodegas at a lower price, making everyone profit. The house plans were beautiful: a four-bedroom home with two master suites, which both had access to the backyard, so if you wanted to come home and not go through the living room or any other space in the house, you could. My mom adored me, so one of those suites was designed specifically for me. Their home had water tanks, one on the roof and another underground. There was also a generator that could provide electricity to the house for up to twenty-four hours. Those two things were a luxury in the DR since there were water shortages and a lot of electricity blackouts, sometimes up to six hours or more. The backyard would have fruit trees, paying homage to my grandparents who had lemon, mango, guava, cherry, orange, and other fruit trees in their backyard. When I recollect those memories at my grandparents, I think of how poor we were, yet we always had fresh fruits and juices that today I take for granted.

CHAPTER III

I left for boot camp on August 1, 1999. I remember my recruiter picked me up at five in the morning so he could take me to the airport. My mother walked me to his car, and gave me a big hug, something that she didn't do often. She gave me a kiss and told me to be myself and to make her proud. I remember crying all the way to the airport. I was scared and anxious of what the future had for me. The recruiter gave me my tickets and the instructions of where to go once I landed in Chicago. Thankfully, it was a direct flight because I am 100 percent sure that I would have gotten lost even having the instructions, because at that moment, I couldn't understand anything.

When I landed in Chicago and walked to the area where all the Navy recruits were supposed to meet, there were about 200 of us! We were all put on yellow buses and were told to just sit and be quiet, and that the ride would be an hour long. I looked around and saw mostly young men and a mixture of races. I also noticed very few had brought anything with them. That was odd to me since I had a small bag with the essentials, like a toothbrush, toothpaste, deodorant, a set of underwear, and white undershirts. We finally made it to Great Lakes, the city where the Navy boot camp is located.

Once the bus parked at this huge building on base, the demeanor of the people in uniform completely changed. They started using curse words, screaming at us to get out of the bus and to get in line. The first line was to make a three-minute phone call to the family to let them know we made it safely. I called my mother, and, of course, I didn't want her to be worried, so I said I was doing okay and that I loved her. Deep down, I was super nervous and wanted to go home. We then moved to another area, where they told us to undress and give them whatever we brought with us. Then we were issued new uniforms, toiletries, and miscellaneous items that we would need while we were in boot camp. All this was happening as we moved from one place to another without having a clue. Several hours passed, with no food and a lot of yelling. To say it was chaotic and frightening would be an understatement, but I had to tell myself that my mom was expecting to see me on the other side.

Even with all that, it didn't really hit home that I had joined the military until I was in line for the next step, getting a haircut. But not just any haircut, they shaved your head almost completely bald! I had a curly mini-afro, and it was all gone. If the purpose was to make you feel like you're not the person you used to be when you arrived, that was accomplished. We finally moved to what would become our living quarters or berthing. By now, it was close to 10:00 p.m., after being up since 4:00 a.m. I was exhausted, hungry, uneasy, and dirty. Unfortunately, I couldn't take a shower and we had to go to sleep.

At 4:00 a.m., reveille sounded. It felt like I had just closed my eyes, and now it was time to get up. That first day, we were trained on the basics, understanding how to indicate left and right in the Navy, which is port and starboard. We learned how to make our beds. Every corner had to have the same setup, neat and tight. Blankets needed to be folded and placed on the bed the same way. Uniformity would be a common theme. We were a division of ninety Sailors; we were as strong as the weakest person, and if anybody messed up or didn't do something, then we all paid for it.

The second day, we started to see what our routine would be like. We would get up at 4:00 a.m. and shower and shave. Shaving was mandatory, even if you didn't have any facial hair, like me; at the time, you had to do it. Then we would go to breakfast, and the way meals worked was the first person would call out when they sat at the table with their tray of food. At that moment, the clock started, the Recruit Division Commander (RDC) would start a stopwatch, and when the last person from the division sat down, the RDC would determine if it was enough time for us to finish eating. I was the last person a few times, and I can tell you that on a couple of occasions, I was only given two to three minutes after shouting, "Last sailor seated!" At the chow hall, we also learned to use our fingers to signal for items on the table. Salt was the index finger, pepper was the index finger and middle finger together, and if you wanted a napkin, you'd cover your mouth with your hand. Of course, this was learned with sweat and on some occasions, tears. The RDC would remember who didn't use the proper signals and make that person or sometimes the entire division do push-ups.

Each division was assigned three RDCs. One was an E-7 Chief Petty Officer, another was an E-6 First Class Petty Officer, and another was an E-5 Second Class Petty Officer. Since we were an all-male division, our three RDCs were male. Chief was of Mexican descent; the first class was white and from the South, and the second class was Black and from the South. The fact that we had such diversity both on pay grade and race was just a coincidence, not the norm. During the next eight weeks of boot camp, each RDC showcased their personality as they tried to teach us how to become Sailors. Chief was the Don Juan. He woke us up at one or two in the morning just to let us know that he just had sex with some sexy lady and that we were gay for "not getting any ass," as he put it. The First Class Petty Officer played the "nice guy" most days, only to feel disrespected at the simplest infraction. The Petty Officer Second Class was always angry and mean and constantly reminded us how dumb we were for joining the Navy instead of going to school.

After each meal, we would either have classwork or drills on how to march. The classes were the hardest because it was a lot of new material, and it was dry. Plus, the classes were after mealtimes, so a lot of us would be fighting for sleep. Dry material combined with waking up at 4:00 a.m. meant that we had to fight to just stay awake. Drinking more water wouldn't help, standing up wouldn't help, and even stretching wouldn't help how tired we all were.

I learned a lot about the Navy that first week, but mostly about discipline and determination. A few things I learned that

I was not expecting was interacting with people from different races and ethnicities. Until boot camp, I had only been around Latinos; this was the first time I was interacting with Black and white Americans. I met people from states that I had never heard about, like North and South Dakota, Wyoming, Iowa, and many more. At first, everyone was quiet and did not talk to others. Some of it was simply that we didn't want to get yelled at, punished, or made to do push-ups for breaking the rules. Another reason had to be the differences we believed the others would have, thinking we'd have nothing in common. Like any situation where you're stressed, nervous, and confused, you start to make bonds with people because they're going through that struggle with you.

I started learning that even if you came from a big city or a small town, you still had a lot of things in common. One of the guys from Iowa shared that he enjoyed doing chores with his mom because it was the only time he felt like he could have one-on-one time with her. That sounded so much like me, yet he was white and lived on a farm while I was Latino and from the city. The biggest shock was realizing that I had an actual fear of African Americans. I had been around them while I delivered goods to the bodegas, yet I embodied fears from what I'd seen on the news. The news displayed African Americans stealing, using, or selling drugs and hurting people. In other words, I only saw the worst in the news, and that's all I knew. In boot camp, I was scared of my brothers. Thankfully, the circumstances didn't give me any other choice but to be open and lean on all the Sailors in my division, because, after all, we were in it together. It didn't matter about our race or background; we had to fight for the common goal and learn about each other as we dealt with the unknown and adversity.

I remember one of my African American brothers telling me the importance of using a washcloth when I showered. Until then, I just rubbed my body with the bar of soap. To me, I was cleaning myself well. But the way he put it was so simple, "When you wash dishes, do you just spray soap on the plate, or do you use something to rub the dry food or oils?" It was like discovering something completely new; I was missing out on truly cleaning my body. It was also the first time some of us heard about financial investing, not from Navy classes, but from a division member who joined the Navy because it would be beneficial for his record later on when he ran for office in his city.

As each day passed, we were more focused and had a better understanding of what military life would be. At the same time, we were deprived of sleep and the stress was mounting to make sure we did well at each event. It was important that you passed each event and milestone in order to graduate on time. The date for my division was October 8. We could only use the phone three times while in boot camp; and each time, I told my mother the date and how much it would mean to me that she was there. That only added more pressure because I knew my mother didn't like flying and couldn't afford to take days off from work. It was going to be a big commitment from her, so in my mind, not graduating on the eighth was not an option no matter how much I was struggling.

One of the events I was required to pass was swim qualifications. Each recruit is placed in an Olympic-sized pool and must dive from a ten-foot platform, swim the length of the pool, and then tread water for three minutes. It sounded reasonable enough for someone who wanted to join the Navy and go to sea. However, I didn't know how to swim, and I was terrified. Our RDC told us that the diver at the bottom would pull you down and you'd have to fight your way up. We thought he was mostly just trying to scare us, and it worked. It made me even more anxious than I already was. Finally, it was my turn to perform the event. To my surprise, the swim test began without any walkthrough or practice first. I kept seeing other recruits approach the platform, hesitant to jump due to nerves, and the RDC would push them off. In the water, a diver grabbed the recruits and dragged them to the side of the pool while all the swim instructors yelled chaotically because they didn't know how to swim.

It was finally my turn. I slowly climbed the steps up to the platform, and I can remember my body shaking, my emotions all over the place, and being almost in tears. Finally, I got to the edge and heard the instructions from the swim instructor, "I will count to three, and then you jump. Once you hit the bottom of the pool, swim to the top. If you don't know how to swim, stay put and a diver will pull you up. Don't struggle with the diver, because they will hit you over the head so hard that you will

go unconscious so your body is relaxed and easier to recover."
As someone who was already worried, this was the last thing I
wanted to hear.

I stepped closer to the edge, and they said, "Are you ready?
Three . . . two . . ." Before he got to three, I felt a push and down
I went! I was incredibly nervous since I didn't know how to
swim, and then I was pushed off without a warning. I felt my
entire life flash by in a split second as I was falling. When I
reached the bottom, I relaxed just like they instructed, but after
a while, I started to fight my way to the top of the pool because
I felt like I had been at the bottom of the pool for ages. Since I
didn't know how to swim, what started as a normal rise to the
top became a frantic fight for air, and I started to kick and move
just like I was told not to. So a diver grabbed me and hit me on
my head, thankfully not hard enough to leave me unconscious,
but it gave me an instant headache. The diver took me to the
top and deposited me on the side of the pool, where I finally felt
safe but very embarrassed. All my peers in the division, along
with other divisions of recruits witnessed the entire event. To
make things worse, my RDC was screaming and calling me a
dumbass and a failure.

The next part of the test was to swim the length of the
pool from one end to the other. I attempted, but after a few
breast strokes, I was tired and not making any progress. I was
also trying to save the minimal amount of energy I still had to
swim to the side of the pool for safety. Seeing as I did not pass
either test, I would have to take extra pool sessions, which really

aggravated my RDC because now I would be missing time with my division to work on academics and drills.

Another week of boot camp passed by, and we came to what was known as "service week." During the week, each recruit was assigned to locations throughout the base to work on different jobs that were either helpful in running the base, providing cleaning services, or some of the more talented recruits played musical instruments for various events. I was assigned to the scullery in the cafeteria, which we called the galley. The only way to describe the scullery was a big hot box where all the dirty dishware went to get washed. It was extremely hot, wet, and gross, and the duty was for eight hours each day. The only good part of service week was that you worked with other divisions, which included females. This was the first opportunity to talk to a female in weeks; it was some type of human contact, and if you both were brave, you could steal a kiss or a feel! I really liked this red-headed female I kept seeing. She was sweet and funny, and we sneaked into the bakery alone to talk, hug, and caress each other. I was really into her body, curvy in all the right places, and I could tell she liked me and wanted to see if there could be something romantic there. We exchanged information about names, division numbers, and berthing numbers, thinking we may have a chance to see each other more.

Service week had the longest days in boot camp. Between waking up at 3:30 am, backbreaking labor, leaning over a hot industrial dishwasher, and being on your feet until 6:00 p.m., it was a complete blur. On top of the extended workday, we returned to the division for marching drills, studying, and cleaning the berthing. It was exhausting.

During the eight weeks of boot camp, we also stood watch in the building where we lived. Watch duties consisted of being in uniform, roving the compartment, ensuring every recruit was sleeping, and monitoring that no one was doing anything they were not authorized to do. Most things were prohibited since nights were meant for rest. Some of the infractions were talking after 10:00 p.m., eating food brought back from the galley, or sneaking into the hallways to meet girls. These watches were usually between 10:00 p.m. and 4:00 a.m., separated into periods of two hours, which meant if you had the 12:00 a.m. to 2:00 a.m., you only slept for two blocks of two hours. Watch duty was unpleasant, but thankfully I got through it without getting in trouble.

During boot camp, we had mail call, which was an exciting time of the week that we'd get to hear from our loved ones and about what was going on out in the real world. Our RDC passed out mail and we would have fifteen minutes at bedtime to read mail and write back. After service week, we had a mail call that Monday, and the RDC was calling names. He finally got to my name, "Recruit Ponciano," and he passed me a letter from my mom. He announced again, "Recruit Ponciano," and handed me a letter from a boot camp friend. Then he said, "What the fuck, Recruit Ponciano, you have a bitch from boot camp sending you mail?" To my surprise, it was a letter from the girl I had met during service week. She used her boot camp address on the envelope, which included her division number. My RDC promptly opened the envelope and recited the entire letter out loud, in which she said how badly she wanted to see me, how she was looking forward to our technical school, and she even described what she wanted to do to me sexually. My RDC was so angry that he made me do what felt like hundreds of pushups, curl-ups, jumping jacks, mountain climbers, and more. Not only was I embarrassed and exhausted, but I was so sweaty that my clothes were soaking wet. Since this occurred after the scheduled time for showers, I had to go to sleep sweaty and smelly. To say I hated that girl for the rest of my time in boot camp was an understatement. I didn't think that she was going to write, and if she did, that she would have left the return address blank. I became a target for the RDCs for the rest of boot camp and paid a price for her oversight for several nights after and whenever the RDC recalled the episode.

CHAPTER IV

My career field in the Navy required a top-secret clearance, and initiating the background check required a lot of information. That meant that I got to make more phone calls than the typical recruit, to attain information from my family and friends, like their birth dates, addresses, and phone numbers. That, coupled with extra swim lessons, meant I was able to transit around the base on my own a lot. This gave me a significant advantage because I was given a level of trust that would continue throughout my career. As I walked from the pool to the administrative building and back to my berthing, I constantly interacted with other RDCs, Officers, and civilians, which helped me learn about showing respect, how to salute, and the intricacies of military honors and traditions.

While I was progressing in academics, unfortunately, my swim lessons were not going well. I was never relaxed enough to learn how to float or do the breaststroke, which was required for the second portion of the test. After weeks of extra training, the swim instructors decided to give me a passing grade and I was cautioned that during the final boot camp exercise, battle stations, I would be put to the test. If I failed at that point, I would be sent back in training to another division, typically back to the third week of boot camp.

It was finally time to go through the final phase of boot camp, where we transitioned from recruits to Sailors. Starting at midnight, each division would face battle stations, a test consisting of twelve events involving academics, problem-solving, and physical strength. The first event was in the pool, where we had to perform life-saving measures, simulating a shipwreck at sea. Of course, I immediately failed, which gave me one of three strikes. I then had the RDCs on high alert, watching my every move. For the rest of the battle stations, I was assigned the "special duty" of carrying twenty wet uniforms in my seabag while we sprinted from one event to another. After only one event, I was already mentally and physically exhausted. The next event was the firing range. The requirement was to shoot above a specific mark, but since my trigger finger had been damaged during a childhood injury, I was not able to shoot the mark expected with the level of accuracy required to pass the event. This was my second of three strikes, which meant that one more strike and I'd be done, resulting in not graduating boot camp. Therefore, my mom would have taken off work and traveled to Great Lakes, only to be disappointed. I kept thinking of her as we were faced with each test. I didn't want to let my mother down, and I didn't want to go through that hell again. Although after each event I was more tired with muscles cramping, I began to see the light at the end of the tunnel.

Around 4:00 a.m., we made it to our last battle station. It was actually one of the easiest events, probably because we knew it was the last test. Our whole division was singing cadence, motivated, and proud. The last battle station was a simulation of a ship taking a hit and the division having to save the ship and us while performing firefighting, flooding, and patching techniques. The level of happiness and relief I felt as they announced, "You have successfully completed your battle station; you're not a recruit anymore, you are a sailor." Those words were the most beautiful thing I had heard in over three months. To make things more symbolic, we were told to return the ball caps we had worn for the past eight weeks. These hats, or covers as we call them in the Navy, said "RECRUIT" in big yellow letters across the front and denoted that you were training to someday become a sailor. After completing battle stations, our newly issued ball caps read, "SAILOR." It was such a culminating moment, I was so proud of accomplishing a goal. It was truly the first time I was tested in my life, and to come out on top was such a high; the kind of high you experience from finishing a marathon or skydiving. You never thought you could do those things, but when you do it and just take that last step or land on the ground, you're in such of level of euphoria.

We then had a few hours to eat a full breakfast, with no dreaded countdown, and could eat all the sweet stuff we hadn't been allowed to eat during boot camp. From there, we marched back to our berthing and were allowed to shower, with no rush or any RDCs yelling at us. We got dressed in our dress white uniforms and marched to the parade hall, where our ceremony was being held. It was so surreal to see family in the stands. Eight weeks had felt like an eternity in an alternate universe. We were instructed to execute our graduation performance without missing a beat, even if we hadn't slept and were distracted by family in the crowd. As we marched in, I looked to see if I could spot my mother, but I didn't until it was time to march from one end of the hall to the other. We had to make a few sharp movements with our heads as we turned, and as I snapped my eyes forward, I spotted my mother, and she was crying. She kept pointing at me, but I couldn't acknowledge her; I couldn't say anything, but I truly felt her joy and how extremely proud she was of me. The ceremony lasted about two hours, which felt like five, but we were done, and I was finally able to hug my mother. She was still crying and telling me that I looked sick because I was so skinny. She couldn't believe that I was not being fed, as she put it. Many of the recruits had lost weight, not due to lack of food, but due to stress, lack of sleep, and learning an entirely new way of life. I really don't remember noticing how much weight I was losing, but I saw my abs showing a lot more and my body was super toned. I probably lost three to five pounds weekly, if not more, from having five to ten minutes to eat, not having snacks throughout the day, and exercising so much. We didn't get to weigh ourselves weekly, but I do remember having to tighten my belt a lot more as the weeks progressed.

After the ceremony, I had to do some administrative paperwork, and then I was told that I could be out in town with my mother as long as I was back in seventy-two hours. My mom drove from New Jersey to Great Lakes with her husband, and we all stayed at a hotel nearby. I think I hit every fast-food joint and restaurant that I had been craving during those eight weeks. She took me to the mall, and I treated myself to a Movado watch, which until that point, was the most expensive thing I had ever owned. I also bought a nice black leather jacket that I still own twenty-three years later. The weekend flew by, and I spent quality time with my mother. I slept a lot before going back and starting the next step in my Navy training, my technical school, referred to as A-school.

That following Monday, I was put on a bus and moved to the other side of the base, where there were several technical schools. My career field was radioman or RM. An RM was a specialist in communications technology that maintained command and control systems on ships, aircraft, and at Navy facilities ashore. During the first week, I became familiar with the new housing area, how to get to the schoolhouse, and where the galley, gym, and library were located. I quickly became oriented with the important places around the base. We were told that we couldn't leave the base, and that it was a privilege to be earned by completing tasks or jobs.

I didn't start school right away. There were several of us on standby because there were too many Sailors who needed to get through RM school at that time. The schoolhouse capacity was only three classes of twenty-five students at a time. While I waited to class up, we performed various duties around the base, like cleaning, standing watch, or guarding different areas. Finally, after three weeks, some of us in holding were put in a group of twenty-five people and told that this group would be our class, and that we would begin training very soon. The instructor assigned a fleet returnee as the class leader, which just meant they had been in the Navy and to at least one duty station, but for some reason were assigned a new career field. Our class leader was a Petty Officer Third Class, E-4, and we were all E-3 and junior. The instructors wanted an assistant, and for some reason they picked me.

Another couple of weeks passed, and we were doing the same duties as before, but still no class start date or timeline. One day, a Petty Officer First Class, E-6, who was one of the instructors, gave us a huge task. He told us the entire class was assigned to clean, move furniture, and paint an entire five-story building. This building would be our new home, and we would have our own rooms with overnight liberty. We were also tasked with creating a watch bill for the different security positions required to run living quarters or barracks. To be honest, it sounded like heaven, the perfect deal. We divided into groups and tackled the building work from the fifth floor down. We'd finish one floor and move on to the next; one team cleaned the rooms, another team painted, and the last team brought the furniture back in. The two other teams cleaned and painted the hallways. The way the building was shaped, the hallways ran in a circle, so you could start cleaning on one end, and the work on each room would follow. We decided to complete each floor in a week, working from 8:00 a.m. to 5:00 p.m., and we were able to hit that target. We also decided to make the third floor our floor. We picked the best furniture since some items were new, but other pieces were repurposed. We also took the cable line that was only supposed to go to each of the lounges on each floor and had the signal split, so we all had cable in our rooms.

After five long weeks, we completed the project and as promised, we were given a liberty card that allowed us to leave the base on a Friday and return before 10:00 p.m. that Sunday. A few weeks after that, we were finally able to attend RM school. Since there were so many students, there were three different shifts. My class ran from 2:00 p.m. to 10:00 p.m. and I was able to get into a routine. During the morning, we went to the gym and performed duties like cleaning the common areas, lounges, laundry room, patios, and walkways around the building. We had to march from the building we lived in to the building where we had class. While marching, it was tradition to sing cadence. This kept us synchronized and gave us energy for the long day.

Two weeks after starting RM school, our career field changed names to "information systems technician," or IT. This was the result of the merger of the RM rating and data processing technicians or DP. DPs operated data processing equipment and performed the administrative tasks for operating computer facilities, including the handling of all classified material passing into or out of computer systems. In class, we started to learn the basics of computers and networks, the Open Systems Interconnection (OSI) model, and different networks, like Local Area Network (LAN) and Wide Area Network (WAN). We also learned about communications systems that operated in different frequency bands, like Extremely High Frequency (EHF), Super High Frequency (SHF), and Ultra High Frequency (UHF). Due to the merger of the RM and DP job fields, the curriculum was new and had a lot of inconsistencies. The class presentation materials were incorrect or not displayed properly, and the students were dismissed so the instructors could figure out the best way forward. Other times, we took an exam on a module, but the questions were incorrect, or the answers provided for the multiple choices were not aligned with the question itself. Since we needed a minimum of an 80 percent average to pass the school, whenever a test was thrown away, we all got a score of 80 percent.

The school was a mess, but we all looked forward to the weekend. One of my friends was a fleet returnee, which was considered cool by all the junior Sailors in our class. My boy got others to pay for him to get a hotel room out in town, while other groups rented four or five rooms and threw parties with food and alcohol. Another thing to do was walk around Gurnee Mills, the huge mall near the base. It was there I saw this girl with beautiful eyes and an amazing smile. I had seen her in the schoolhouse, but at those moments I hadn't had the time to say anything. It was at the mall that I finally had the courage to approach her and say something. She smiled so big and had this Southern accent that I loved.

Ashley and I quickly became a couple. I don't think that we actually made it official by my asking her, "Do you want to be my girlfriend?" But we just started acting like a couple. We told others we were together and held hands whenever we could. We also started using those rooms that my boy used to get. He didn't care if we used his hotel room, because most of the time he would end up in another girl's room. We were both so innocent and immediately embarked on what was known as "A-school love." That kind of love was so powerful because you had all these factors contributing to the attachment. You were both away from family for the first time, both coming from eight to ten weeks of no human contact and exploring this new world. It was the thought of a future together, and for some of us, the first time we fell in love.

This was my first time being with someone that was not Latina. I was also in love with *Baywatch*'s icon Pamela Anderson, and my A-school love was a damn near mirror image. We talked about what the future would be, and how much we cared about each other. Ashley was a week or two behind me in classes, so I had to leave before her and go to my first duty station. I really liked her, and I wanted us to work out, but I had a feeling that her parents didn't approve of our relationship, specifically her dad. She was from the South, and even in the year 2000, racism was still prominent.

About two weeks before my class was scheduled to graduate, we got the chance to pick our first command in the Navy. The instructor said that we would make selections based on our ranking in the class, but a few days later that changed. As a collective, we all scored low on an exam, of which a passing score was needed to move on to the next module. He made the decision to use that order instead of the overall class ranking. I was upset because I was ranked number two overall in class; but based on only the exam, I was number twelve. I watched people ahead of me select orders to commands that I would have loved, like the aircraft carrier *John F. Kennedy* out of Florida. Another student picked a Naval Communications Station in Rota, Spain. The next sailor got Naples, Italy. I really hoped for an overseas duty station so I would be able to travel and see the world. Finally, it was my time to pick. I looked at the list, and there was nothing that interested me. Then I asked my instructor which command would provide the opportunity to be able to learn both sides of our career field, networks and communications. He said to pick a guided missile destroyer or DDG, because it is a small crew, and you'd get to learn everything about the IT field. The list had a few DDGs out Norfolk, San Diego, Florida, and even Japan. I looked at the instructor and the list, looked to see a reaction from him as I read each command. I even started to read some of them out loud, without even knowing, which made him upset. He told me to hurry up and pick or he would pick for me. My next question was which one was the newest DDG, and he said the USS *Cole* (DDG-67), which was commissioned in 1996. Because of this, I selected the USS *Cole*, whose homeport was Norfolk, Virginia. After my pick, for whatever reason, he stopped allowing others to pick and just made the picks himself. There were a lot of upset and disappointed Sailors, but the instructor was king.

Once I made peace with the fact that I was not going overseas, I was excited to be going somewhere I had never been. Ashley also picked orders, and she was assigned to a ship in Gaeta, Italy. We told each other that we would be able to work, even in a long-distance relationship. Before we graduated, my sponsor from the USS *Cole* contacted me. We talked about me taking leave before reporting to the ship, the ship's deployment schedule, and my career goals. We were authorized to take up to four weeks of leave from school en route to our duty stations.

I decided to take three weeks since I didn't have enough leave days saved up to take more. My girlfriend was going to meet me in New Jersey so she could meet my mother and brother. I left Great Lakes in February of 2000, after graduating from A-school.

Being home after not seeing my mother for over six months was so refreshing. I ate her delicious Dominican food, slept in my own bed, and caught up with my neighborhood friends. It was exactly what I needed before I reported to my first command. After a week at home, my girlfriend came to visit. My mother loved her even though she didn't speak any Spanish. Since my mother did not speak English, I translated every conversation, which was challenging but also adorable. Ashley loved my mother's cooking, especially the white rice; she just smiled and looked at my mom and said yum! My mother always told me how much she enjoyed the way I looked at Ashley and smiled. Very little conversation really happened between them but I really loved the interest they showed in each other. My mother always wanted me to be with a Dominican woman, so I was extremely surprised that she was so happy with Ashley. I took her around Union City, where I grew up, to see my high school, the bodega where I ordered steak and cheese or a tuna sandwich for lunch, the local movie theater across the street from my house, and areas in New York City. We continued to talk about how we would make it work once I moved to Virginia and she moved to Italy.

After a week, she went home to finish her leave in Georgia, and I stayed for what I thought was going to be a week with my mother. A couple of days later, I received a call from my sponsor on the USS *Cole* telling me that I should report to my command a week early because the ship was due to go underway for six weeks. He explained it would be beneficial for me to be on the underway before we embarked on a seven-month deployment in August. I didn't know a lot about the Navy at that point; I felt like it was an order, so I didn't question it. I immediately called the Navy travel agency, and they adjusted my tickets to leave New Jersey the very next day. I hugged my mother and brother and said goodbye, not knowing when I would see them next. My mother was planning to retire in the Dominican Republic later that year, so it would be more difficult to visit her. It was always her dream to go back, so I didn't want to let her know how much I was going to miss her and how lonely I would feel without her. I guess I felt like I had to be a man now that I was in the Navy.

CHAPTER V

At the airport, everyone looked at me and thanked me for my service. It was customary to report to your next duty station in the dress uniform for the season, and since I was reporting to the USS *Cole* directly after I arrived at the Norfolk airport in Virginia, I flew in my dress whites uniform. While the uniform looked very sharp, it got dirty very easily, especially when carrying a seabag and other luggage. In March of 2000, I landed at Norfolk International Airport. My sponsor arranged for someone else to pick me up, but since I'd never been to Norfolk, I was lost and confused. I eventually found the sailor, and she drove me to Norfolk Naval Station and dropped me at the pier. She told me the USS *Cole* was at berth four, and to tell the officer of the deck (OOD) that I was a new check in, and they would know what to do. I got to the brow and rendered a proper salute to the American flag before requesting permission from the OOD to come onboard. A Petty Officer First Class was the OOD, and he said that the section leader was expecting me. A Chief Petty Officer showed up and took me down to radio, which is the area for ITs onboard a ship.

Although I spoke with my sponsor about four times over the phone, based on my first name, the command thought I was a female, so I didn't have a rack in the male berthing. The duty IT, who was a Petty Officer Third Class, located an empty rack and clean linens for me. I didn't sleep well, since the berthing was so cold and I was so anxious.

The next morning, I put on my dress whites uniform again and ensured I was perfectly shaved and ready to check in. I met my sponsor; she was a female Petty Officer Second Class who was Hispanic as well. That made me feel more at home. I felt like she would understand me, coming from the same kind of background, and also would help me understand my job better since I was still not comfortable with my English. I knew I could ask her in Spanish and I would get a breakdown in my native language. I then met my Leading Petty Officer (LPO), IT1 Bloodsaw, who was a black First Class Petty Officer. He was super funny and welcoming. I spent most of the day meeting everyone from my shop. They were all excited to be getting underway the next day, and even more so to experience a port visit. I found out later that we were pulling into Miami for four days, and we had maximum liberty, even as junior Sailors.

Later that day, I checked in with the command Master Chief, who was the highest-ranking enlisted sailor onboard the ship. He welcomed me to the USS *Cole* and impressed upon me to make my family proud by always doing the right thing. I met other Chiefs and Officers who led different programs, like the command fitness leader; this Chief was very fit and spoke about how important fitness was to the Navy but also for me as a man. Then we met the command financial specialist; she talked to me about how important it was to be smart with my money, and that I was not going to make a lot as a Seaman, so having a budget would benefit me greatly. I also met the Drug and Alcohol Program advisor, Urinalysis Program coordinator, and others whom I would need to interact with during my tour.

Each person seemed very welcoming and eager to help me, to make me feel part of the *Cole* family, and to provide support when I needed it. I changed into blue coveralls, the Navy's working uniform, so I could get to work and start learning about communications procedures and other shipboard duties.

On my first day, I got to set up the communication paths that we would use while out at sea. With more senior IT supervision, I set up super high frequency to high frequency circuits. These circuits ensured that our ship was able to communicate with other ships and shore stations and transmit data for the use of the internet and email. Within the first seventy-two hours of arriving at a ship, every sailor was required to memorize routes from the berthing to topside in case of an emergency. I was shown how to evacuate my work area and berthing in case of fire, flooding, or any other emergency. I walked through the routes a few times, and even backward once. The last evolution was done blindfolded, to simulate a power outage and the possibility of complete darkness so that I really understood the area and all the turns required to get to safety. After a long day, around 5:00 p.m. I was told that I was done for the day. I went to the galley and had dinner, and sitting there by myself I thought about all the new adventures I was about to embark on. I went out to sea for the first time, hit my first Navy port, and realized that the ship would become my workspace, family, and home.

I headed down to my berthing and moved to a different bed, which was the area where all the other ITs lived. The way the beds were built was like bunk beds, but three high. Each bed, which we called a coffin rack, lifted up, and there was storage space inside for each sailor's personal belongings. I was on the top rack, so I had a bit more space because it did not have a top cover like the other racks. The bottom rack had the middle rack on top of it and the middle rack had the top rack on top of it, so the space was very small; mine was very open in comparison. There was wiring and tubes hanging down, but unlike the other racks that were enclosed, I had enough space to sit up. In addition to the coffin rack, I also had a standup locker. Not a full locker, as you might see in high school, but more of a half locker as you would find at a fitness center. Since the ship was also my home, I had all my belongings, clothes, and shoes with me. Thankfully, the ship had a storage location, called a seabag locker. I was able to safely store some of my belongings, like winter clothes, shoes, and excess uniform items. After I organized my storage compartments, I made my bed with more comfortable linens than the sandpaper sheets and thin wool blanket issued by the ship. I had hoped to sleep a bit more comfortably with nicer bedding on the four-inch-thick mattress.

On day two, I woke up early so I could shower, shave, and eat breakfast before 7:00 a.m. I wanted to be in the shop and ready for instructions as early as possible. After reviewing the schedule for the day, I saw there were a few evolutions that I did not have experience in. One of them was called "sea and anchor," which is a shipboard condition set for ships entering or exiting ports. This evolution required manning multiple watch stations throughout the ship, like the bridge, forecastle, fantail, engineering plant, aft steering, damage control central, and line handlers. I was going to be part of the line landers on the forward area of the ship, called the forecastle or fo'c'sle.

We left the pier around 8:30 a.m. and quickly made our way south. The sea and anchor detail was uneventful, but I observed a lot since I was learning under instruction or UI. Since I wasn't yet qualified for the duties, I did my best to absorb and learn. I was not allowed to touch anything unless I was being supervised. Once sea and anchor was secured, I returned to the radio shop, where I was informed I'd be working the night shift from 7:00 p.m. to 7:00 a.m.. I decided to wait until lunch was served so I could have something to eat before I turned in to rest before overnight watch. I remember it was taco Tuesday, which to me tasted delicious. I now believe I was just very hungry because ship food is mediocre at best. When you're feeding 250 people, it is a nearly impossible task to craft delectable food. I got down to berthing, took a shower, and climbed into my rack. My alarm went off at 6:00 p.m. and I got dressed, brushed my teeth, and headed to radio. The first night of watch was rough because my body was trying to acclimatize to sleeping during the day and being awake at night.

The job of an IT is mostly reactive. When a communications system or network is not functioning properly, we fix it. It is an impossible task to predict outages or get ahead of malfunctions, especially when it comes to the network. The routine was the same for most days out to sea, and I was getting the hang of it. Twice a week, we would perform general quarters, or GQ, where we practiced emergency responses to fire, flooding, chemical gas, or enemy attacks, like inbound missiles or torpedoes. These drills were critical in everyone's role during an emergency, the understanding of system capabilities, sailor knowledge, and building muscle memory. My first general quarters station was Repair Locker 2, where we were assigned to the forward part of the ship for repairs, firefighting, and de-flooding. My GQ position was "boundary man," with the task of setting boundaries during emergency flooding or fire. The goal was to ensure nothing spread from one compartment to another. "Watertight integrity" is defined as closures or fittings that prevent the ingress of water to certain compartments. This original watertight integrity may be reduced or destroyed through enemy action.

I remember my first GQ in Repair Locker 2. I had a young fireman, who had more experience, walk with me to each of the boundaries I had to set. I had to truly understand how to read locations on the ship and take ownership of the cards that were assigned to me. In those cards, I was assigned four zones that I had to set boundaries for. I had to also understand what each "material conditions" meant, which dictate what doors and other fittings can be opened, balancing ease of use with the need to protect the ship. Each of these objects was labeled with an X, Y, or Z as appropriate to the condition it had to be closed under. Condition X-ray was set during the day while in port or at anchor and involved the least restrictions. Condition Yoke was typical while a ship is at sea, or at night while in port, while condition Zebra was used during GQ.

Every sailor on the ship was expected to perform GQ duties, to be knowledgeable and capable of emergency responses to protect the ship, and to qualify for cardiopulmonary resuscitation (CPR). In addition to basic firefighting and CPR, I was also trained on how to control and transport fire hoses in the event of a fire. Day after day of repeating the same drills felt like Groundhog Day, but it was exciting for me to learn about the Navy, the vulnerabilities of the ship, and most of all, form a greater sense of purpose and belonging. We were learning so much about how to fight the ship and how to perform in different environments.

My LPO had this amazing way to make you feel like you were family, that he had your back no matter what, and that he would always care about you. For me it was the way he would talk to people, humble and with care, the way he would not ask you to do anything he wouldn't do himself. He was funny, warm, and cared for us like we were his children. Thanks to the advice of my LPO, IT1 Bloodsaw, I became a sponge for knowledge. He used to say, "Every day is an opportunity to learn, and today is the best day to learn something new." Thanks to him, my mind was in constant receiving mode and I was always looking for new opportunities to improve my knowledge and skills. As much as I enjoyed being part of a repair locker, I really wanted to be in radio during GQ. Staying in radio was a huge benefit because during GQ we practiced real-life events and really trained on how to still have communications regardless of the casualty. After multiple reps and sets and forming my baseline knowledge in the repair locker, I finally asked my LPO how I could move to radio for GQ. He replied that I needed to get qualified for the radio GQ position, which was tech control communicator. He recommended that I become so knowledgeable and reliable that I would be critical to the division's success. I really took that advice to heart and put my head down to be my best self. I would think about what Ashley was doing in Italy while I got used to the ship life. We talked here and there but I missed her so much that I would try not to call often.

After three weeks of drills underway and very little sleep, we made it to Miami. I understood the ceremonial aspect of performing sea and anchor detail in my working white uniform but was also concerned about my uniform getting dirty, and not having the money to replace it. That feeling quickly faded once I saw the beautiful houses in Miami harbor, majestic cruise ships, beautiful people walking around, and Sailors working together to perform their duties. My feelings quickly turned into excitement and anticipation because once we were moored on the pier, I would be able to clean up and go on liberty at my very first port call. After we secured from sea and anchor, we mustered as a division back in radio for a liberty brief. Our LPO trained us on how to represent the Navy out in town and appropriate behavior while in a port. He told us to have fun but also that we were all adults trusted to defend this beautiful country, and as such we owed it to our family and the American people to behave and come back to the ship safely. He ensured we all knew when liberty expired for each pay grade, which was the time we had to be onboard the ship at the end of the night. For an E-1 Seaman recruit, like me, liberty expired at 2:00 a.m..

I was so happy and right away started looking for liberty buddies. We were required to have at least three Sailors in our group, with a designated nondrinker, which was me. It made sense since I was the only one under twenty-one in my group. We all showered and got dressed in nice comfortable clothes and hit the streets. Our ship provided shuttle buses that would take us from the pier to downtown and South Beach. We decided as a group that the first stop was to find some food. Since we were all junior pay grades, our budget was very small. We looked for a fast-food restaurant that we had been missing during the underway. Burger King was the consensus, and I will tell you that I had the most delicious Whopper I ever tasted. Even to this day, I remember that exact mouthwatering experience.

Next, it was time to find a spot by the beach to have drinks. We got to a restaurant in South Beach early in the evening and were seated at a nice table. The restaurant was also a bar, in a great location for foot traffic, and not too fancy. The amount of beautiful people from all backgrounds and nationalities was intriguing and gave me life. To see that melting pot and how beautiful people can be from all walks of life was a high I would continue to seek for the rest of my life through both Navy and personal travel. We kept seeing shipmates pass by who talked to us about the amazing time they were having, how expensive everything was, or how hot it was. As it got closer to 10:00 p.m., the street became even busier. We continued drinking and enjoying appetizers from the restaurant. As the dedicated sober guy, my drink of choice was juice and soda. Since it was our first night out, we called it a night at midnight just to make sure we understood how long it took to get back to the ship. We also wanted to set a positive tone for the rest of the time in Miami. Before I hit my rack, I would always try to call Ashley. Most of the time, we wouldn't connect. She was six hours ahead, so a lot of the time she was still sleep or already at work.

During our port visit, we met some amazing people (beautiful ladies, an old lady who was a vendor in the street, and a Cuban middle-aged guy who ran the panaderia, aka bakery), had some delicious food and drinks, and caught up on some much-needed rest before getting back to sea. When we got underway, there were another three weeks of shipboard evolutions, emergency exercises, learning, sleep deprivation, adjustment to rough seas, ship food, and a full schedule. We finally made it back to our home port of Norfolk, Virginia. We were told that we could take leave for up to fourteen days before we were to leave on our seven-month deployment. Unfortunately, I only had five days of leave saved up. IT1 Bloodsaw still allowed me to take seven days of leave because he knew I would be able to save leave days while on deployment. I didn't have a lot of money, so I asked my mother for money to take the Greyhound bus to see her one last time before leaving. That ride was so long; we stopped at about ten locations between Norfolk and Times Square, New York.

While at home, my mother discussed with me that she was planning to retire in the Dominican Republic. She was able to save enough money to build her dream house there, start a small business, and have money left to pay the bills for six months. Her dream was to always go back and her husband wanted to start a business as well. I was sad since she would be so far away from me, but also extremely proud of her and her accomplishments. She had always dreamed about going back to her island to be near family and the culture she loved. For those seven days, I focused on connecting with my mother and dear friends as much as possible. I made an effort to go out during the day and see friends and family so when my mother made it home from work after 6:00 p.m., I was home and we could have dinner together. Saturday morning I made her breakfast— scrambled eggs, bacon, and toast for her, her husband, and my brother. It was a small gesture to tell her to relax and that I loved her. We called Ashley, and they talked to each other using me as the translator, but my mother asked a few questions about how things were going and said we would make it work. It was the first time I really thought about that.

Funny enough, in that visit I saw Stephanie's mom at the supermarket and we both recognized each other. I gave her a big hug and she kissed me goodbye. We both had that smile of two people reminiscing about the past. I wonder why I didn't try her again, but I didn't. I also saw a few other people from high school and a couple of my cousins that lived in New York City. Seven days is never enough time to see family, especially when you want to give each enough time to have a meaningful conversation.

Around this time, Ashley and I broke it off. The lack of communication was taking a toll, and the realization that it would be a long time before we saw each other again was also weighing heavily. Before we hurt each other by cheating or anything else, we decided to end it. Looking back, it was very mature for our age. This was an early lesson on love in the military that I would reference throughout my life.

CHAPTER VI

In August of 2000, Bill Clinton was the president, and we were ready to start our deployment on the USS *Cole* to the Mediterranean. We were told that our first port visit would be Barcelona, Spain. As someone who joined the Navy to see the world, this was exciting news. The day before we were set to sail, my LPO let us know that if we got more people qualified to stand watch, then we could go to three sections. This would make a huge difference since 90 percent of the time ITs worked twelve hours on and twelve hours off. In your twelve off hours, you had to budget time to sleep, workout, study, and contribute to all shipboard evolutions and drills. Within a week, we had enough Sailors qualified to adjust our schedule into three sections. The three shifts were 6:00 a.m. to 2:00 p.m., 2:00 p.m. to 10:00 p.m., and 10:00 to 6:00 a.m.. This meant eight hours on, and sixteen hours off. I was in the third section, 10:00 to 6:00 a.m.. I loved the hours since most people were sleeping, and the watch was quiet. All we had to worry about were daily tasks.

After about two weeks, we pulled into Barcelona, Spain. The harbor was beautiful, the weather was perfect, and our excitement could not be contained. During the sea and anchor detail, I noticed how small boats from Spain would moor right next to our ship so we could properly dispose of hazardous materials. I had duty the first day we were in port. Duty meant I had to remain on board with about 100 other Sailors from my duty section for a period of twenty-four hours. The crew that remained on duty ensured all the major watch stations were manned properly in the event of an emergency. It was also the same people who would get the ship underway in case there was a reason to rapidly pull out of port. While in port overseas, we would be in three-section duty, splitting the crew of 100 Sailors into three teams to trade off covering down on shipboard duties. Thankfully, my small group of friends were all in section three, so it made things easier as far as having liberty buddies.

While in Spain, the liberty for my pay grade ended at 2:00 p.m.. We were delighted that the drinking age was eighteen since we all wanted delicious sangria alongside our paella. While on liberty, my friends and I walked and explored everywhere. We also got to visit the 1992 Olympic stadium and the surrounding areas. We took in the local culture, tasted so many foods, and experienced everything Barcelona had to offer.

While in Barcelona, I remembered another piece of advice I received from IT1 Bloodsaw. He said to always take at least one Morale, Welfare, and Recreation (MWR) tour. MWR is a Navy organization that hosts day trips to explore a city without all the alcohol and distractions. Plus, it was the best way to take pictures to send home since he always emphasized that our family was proud of what we did. Thus, we should show them the amazing places we got to experience. Since we were in port for four days, I really got to enjoy the city and the nightlife. I got to dance every night, and since I spoke Spanish, I also served as the translator for my shipmates, which was fun and interesting.

Our next port was France, and to be honest, I really don't remember the city. It could have been Monaco because what I do remember was that it was very expensive. It was also a much shorter port visit, but I do remember eating in a few restaurants, visiting a lot of beautiful beaches, and seeing gorgeous people. This was the timeframe when I started to break out of my shell and experience a new confidence in talking to women. Maybe it was the liquid courage or the understanding that I would never see these foreign ladies again. Whatever it was, with the increased body language, smiles, and easy conversation I was encountering, my confidence grew.

After that, we were back underway for a few days and we pulled into Split, Croatia. It felt like we were hitting a port every three or four days, which was awesome, but also meant I was broke. As an E-2, our salary was about $462 every two weeks. I still managed to have a lot of fun. I also took one of the MWR trips that took us to Venice, Italy, which was one of the best decisions I made as a young sailor. It was a seven-hour drive from Split to Venice, so we stayed overnight in Venice. The trip included transportation, the hotel, meals, and sightseeing. During this trip, I found myself looking at a lady onboard the *Cole* a lot more. Her smile and sense of humor really came out while we were on liberty. On the ship, we were all mostly about business since there was always so much work to accomplish. I knew that she was interested in, or dating someone else. I ended up hooking up with someone else during the trip and she was beautiful and sexy, but I was mostly thinking about the other lady. We would lock eyes here and there and smile, but nothing more. She had her group of friends, and I had mine. Rose was higher ranking than me, so that was also an obstacle in my eyes.

On the night we returned from Venice, we all decided to go out in Split. That day was a holiday for the city, so there was only one hip-hop club open, which meant that everyone from the ship was there. Most importantly, the lady I liked was there too. I took the opportunity to ask Rose to dance, and she loved to dance and could really move. We were bumping and grinding for most of the night, but she had a few admirers. When it was time to go back to the ship, we all jumped on the bus, and I saved her a seat. Rose sat next to me, and we talked about this one guy who wanted to get with her. He kept interrupting us or would just say something random to get her attention. We made it back to the ship, and as we walked down the pier to the brow of the ship, she was focused on others.

I waited in a spot where I knew Rose had to pass by on the way to her berthing, even if it was late since it was past 2:00 a.m. Rose saw me, and I told her how much I enjoyed dancing with her. I also told her I loved her smile and that I hoped to see her again out in town. Rose told me that she was seeing someone, but that she also liked me. As we spoke, we unconsciously moved closer to each other while also keeping a lookout of our surroundings. Then we shared a quick, passionate kiss, and both turned the other way, quickly understanding that we had just broken a rule onboard a Navy ship. We were not allowed to have any physical contact with the other sex. Rose held my hand for a little while. I slapped her ass and she smiled and walked away.

I was so hyped that I could hardly sleep, but I also knew that the next day we were going underway again. A couple more days of training and drills and the opportunity for more learning about Navy life.

Just as soon as we were underway, we were at our next port visit, Malta. Malta was a beautiful small island between Sicily and Tunisia. When our ship was navigating the port, I saw old castles and structures off in the distance. The way the port was set up, there was an elevated structure directly next to the pier, which looked like the side of a wall for a castle. On the upper walkway, there were dozens of beautiful ladies looking down at our ship and pointing to the sailor they liked or wanted attention from. It was like a scene from a movie, and something I had never experienced. After the ship was moored, and sea and anchor was secured, we were ready to change out of our working whites so we could shower and hit the town.

IT1 Bloodsaw could tell we were super excited, and he made sure to remind us that we were representing the Navy and to be on our best behavior. He told us the local ladies wanted to have a good time, not get married, so use protection and don't fall in love. He was so adamant about protection that he made us go to medical and get condoms before we left the ship on liberty. I really wanted to see Rose from the ship in port since I didn't get to see her a lot while underway. I worked nights, and she worked days, so our schedules never lined up. She must have had plans with her boyfriend onboard because I didn't see her on any of the days while we were in Malta. So my focus switched to the local ladies. The women from Malta were a rare combination of Italian, Egyptian, and British, plus the ratio of women to men was about five to one.

My group of friends took the bus from the pier to the city. While we waited for the bus, I was able to take a picture of the ship from the castle and the entire ship was visible, especially the forward area, where the hull number, 67, could be seen. It was a disposable camera and when we made it to the city, I dropped it off and got the photos developed. Thankfully, they were done in forty-five minutes and I sent a few to my mother right away. The spot where the bus dropped us off was the middle of the city and we just wandered around. There were two main streets and we chose the one on the right, which had lots of restaurants and shops. We had our meals, bought some souvenirs, and just chilled until about 8:00 p.m. when we decided to get back to the middle of town and head to the left street. Well, we hit the jackpot of fun since that street was full of bars, clubs, and even strip clubs. We hit a couple of bars and then hit the club with the biggest line.

Inside of the club were many of my male shipmates and beautiful Maltese women. Quickly, I was on the dance floor bouncing from one beautiful woman to another. We didn't have to rush, since our Commanding Officer rewarded the crew for our great behavior in other ports with more relaxed liberty expiration, so we all had to be back by 6:00 a.m. if we didn't have a request chit for staying overnight at a hotel in town. Around 1:00 a.m. we started to focus on who we were hoping to end the night with. I had the attention of this beautiful lady, who was a mixture of Egyptian and British. She took me to her place and my boy and his girl came with us. We had our fun and woke up around 5:45 a.m., not enough time to make it to the ship. Thankfully, I had the number into radio and I called, spoke with my LPO, and he said, "Glad that you guys are ok and thank you for calling, just make it back to the ship before eight so I can see you in person and then you can go back out." So we did just that—met him and let him know about our amazing day, showered, and slept until three or four, and then got ready to hit the town and repeat the same adventure. This time we met different women and had fun with many others. It was a wild port visit.

I had to work one of the days in Malta. My new job on the ship was food service attendant (FSA) or cranking. My job was to help with the serving of food for the crew, cleaning the galley or cafeteria, and cleaning the kitchen area for all three meals. Because I was always on time and my uniform was always clean, I was moved from the enlisted galley to the officer galley or wardroom. I learned a lot of etiquette, like how to pour water, how to place utensils, what utensils were used for what foods, and a lot more. I had to walk up and down the ladders a lot for the duties as FSA, which was exhausting. We left Malta, and it was one of the most memorable three or four days of my young life. A few days while underway, I was going down the ladder to workout and the ship rocked and I lost my footing and hit my knee really bad. I couldn't go up and down as much, so I was replaced as an FSA and came back to radio. About a week after leaving Malta, we had to do the Suez Canal transit. The Suez Canal is a human-made waterway that cuts north-south across the Isthmus of Suez in Egypt. The Suez Canal connects the Mediterranean Sea to the Red Sea, making it the shortest maritime route to Asia from Europe, and it can take hours or days to cross due to the traffic of other ships and how deep or wide a ship could be. It was a long day but really cool to see two countries on each side of the ship after so many days of just water around us. After transiting the canal, we were heading to the Middle East. I can't remember if it was United Arab Emirates or Bahrain, but that was the direction the ship was heading.

One night during the underway, we had a fuel spill that caused the ship to go into general quarters. It was a very dramatic and panicked experience, but my shipmates and I were able to close all the hatches and set Zebra, which provided the greatest degree of subdivision and watertight integrity to the ship. It is the maximum state of readiness for the ship's survivability system. What was shocking to me was how quickly we set Zebra. We kept having drills before that day and not meeting the mark as far as setting Zebra throughout the ship. The maximum time should be nine minutes, yet we were doing it anywhere between twelve to fifteen minutes. The Commanding Officer was extremely upset and he came over the 1 Main Circuit or 1MC, which is the primary public address system used on all US Navy ships. He let us know how disappointed he was and how we were going to continue to drill all day and night until we got it right. Thankfully, the night of the oil spill we set Zebra in less than eight minutes and thirty seconds, and the fire party and engineering department did a great job on not only stopping the spill but also cleaning the area affected. Unfortunately, this meant that we had to refuel sooner than expected and we didn't have an oiler ship for us to do an UNREP. An underway replenishment, or UNREP, is a broad term that applies to all methods of transferring fuel, ammunition, supplies, and personnel from one ship to another while underway. I was lucky to be the IT who set up the laptop for the projector in the wardroom, where the CO and other Officers discussed where we could go to with the amount of fuel we had and staying in the route to accomplish our mission. A few locations were discussed and after inputs from the 5th fleet commander, boss of the region, the decision was made to go to Aden, Yemen.

It was October 12, 2000; we were told that we were going to be setting the sea and anchor detail around 8:00 a.m. and we would refuel for the time that we moor until about six hours later. The pier we were going to moor to was a small refueling station in the middle of the harbor. The best way I could describe it is a harbor in a U-shape with land all around it and the small pier in the middle of it all. We were going to moor with the ship facing land, but our Commanding Officer demanded that we moor with the ship facing the water in case anything happened. As we got into the harbor and the ship moved to get in position, we were all shocked at how bad the harbor looked, from Yemeni's ship sinking to very old infrastructure. The place just looked rundown. We finally moored and we secured the sea and anchor detail. I headed to radio and started training one of the deck seamen who wanted to become an IT. About an hour later, the Executive Officer came over the 1MC and announced that we were refueling so quickly that he was going to order early chow for those in the sea and anchor detail. This way, we would eat and be ready to do our responsibilities as sea and anchor members.

I, another IT, and the seamen we were training headed to the chow line to eat. They started walking to the head of the line and I said, "Nobody is going to believe that an IT has the next watch," so I stayed back. About five minutes later, I heard the loudest sound I had ever heard in my life, and my body moved back and forth and hit the wall of the ship and the person I was talking to. I was in shock, thinking what just happened; my mind right away thought it was an explosion on the refueling pier, but if that would have been the case then I would have been dead since I was standing on the starboard or right side of the ship, which was the side we were refueling. As I started to get my bearings, I saw this ball of smoke and fire coming in my direction, like in the movies. So scared of what might have happened, I started to head to the aft or back of the ship with others to try to leave the inside or skin of the ship. Before we could reach the last hatch, the Executive Officer was coming from the outside of the ship and he was screaming, "We were hit by a small boat with a bomb; go to your general quarters station and tell everyone you pass by since the 1MC is not working." I instantly turned around and headed to radio, which was about 30 feet from the spot on the ship where the bomb went off.

As I was moving through the ship, I saw people moving in different directions and others just crying. I got to radio and my Chief Petty Officer told me, "I have an Alpha and a

Bravo personnel (two sides of the safe), you go to your old repair locker and help in whatever damage control efforts." I understood that she was letting me know that she and two others were capable of doing emergency destruction of all classified materials if the Commanding Officer ordered them to do so due to the imminent danger of the ship sinking. I understood that she was getting ready to abandon ship. I headed to my old repair locker, Repair 2, in the forward area of the ship. I saw an Officer or Chief, I can't remember, but I know the person was wearing a khaki bell, which indicated it was one or the other, and he told me, "Go back aft to Repair 3 and help there with the damage control efforts." I moved back aft and closed every hatch as I moved from one area to another. Around the area of the scullery was the section of the dining facility where pots, pans, and dishes were scrubbed and rinsed. I found a body there, covered only by a blanket. For some reason, I decided to uncover the person and see who it was; it was one of my friends that I used to go on liberty with. Gunn was a signalman and only twenty-two years old. He was extremely funny, caring, and had one of the most beautiful smiles you could ever witness. He was part of my crew, and his body was full of metal pieces, head cut where you could see his brain, and blood everywhere. The only way I recognized who he was, since his body was swollen, was by his name tape on his coveralls. I couldn't believe it; he was such a big part of our crew. He was someone that always wanted to try new things, who was not afraid to talk to girls in our port visits, and someone who was always willing to help. My heart felt like it was in my mouth and I couldn't breathe.

I felt my knees get weak and I was on my knees without knowing. I started crying and shaking my head, saying to myself, "I don't want to be here; I want to see and be close to my mother." I was overwhelmed with emotions, fear, and sadness. After a few minutes, I felt someone tap my shoulder. I looked back and the person said, "Unfortunately, he is gone; we need to save the ship and our shipmates." I know that those words might sound harsh to others, but at that moment it was what I needed. I stood up and headed back to Repair 3 to do what I was trained to do. Once I got to the locker, I saw people injured and others looking for guidance on what to do next. I was still crying and shaking, but I was eager to help and do whatever it took to keep the safe afloat and my shipmates safe. I was told to go to a specific area with three other Sailors, with a P-100; a P-100 pump is a commercial, diesel-engine driven portable pump designed for firefighting and limited dewatering functions aboard ships. Our responsibility was to ensure the pump would work properly and move it to another area of the compartment if needed.

After about an hour of just making sure the pump was working properly, I was told that I needed to go back to the locker and bring buckets to take water out of another compartment. We were simply pushing water closer to the pump so the water could be removed faster. For the next three or four hours, I was just a runner. I was going to any place I was needed and moving equipment to where it was needed. As things started to stabilize, I decided to look for the rest of the ITs from my shop and the Sailors I was really close with. I made it back to the biggest area, where the ship was hit, which was the chow hall and galley line.

I got as close as I could without falling into the hall or getting electrocuted. I saw a few of my shipmates missing limbs, with their heads chopped off, or with shards of metal all around their body. It was a visual that will haunt me for the rest of my life, but I had to make sure my people were ok. I continued to look for more people. I would find someone and keep it in my mind and kind of have a countdown, and I would say to myself that's IT number 7 out of 12 and keep looking. I even looked for the girl I liked and had kissed. I found her and we hugged and cried. I was so happy to see her alive and not injured. I made my way to the back of the ship, and in the flight deck many of the injured were being treated and prepared for evacuation to local hospitals. My LPO was one of those; he had a broken jaw and needed medical treatment. Even with his injury, he was still trying to give instructions and be encouraging.

Another fifteen to twenty of my shipmates were evacuated. The doctors onboard diagnosed what was wrong and how it could be treated onboard or if it required extensive medical care. As the hours passed, the adrenaline levels were getting lower and tiredness started to creep up. I was exhausted, both physically and emotionally. The main corpsman, or doctor, onboard asked if he could get some volunteers to help him go through the bodies of those that passed away and get their personal belongings so they can be turned in to their families. I really thought that was a nice gesture that I would have liked my mother to have if I was the one that was killed. I helped with two bodies, and I still remember today what it's like to touch a dead body, the smell of blood mixed with metal and fuel. Although

I still have nightmares about that, I would do it again because I know what it meant to the families of my shipmates.

After sitting down to gather my thoughts for a few minutes and looking at my friends looking exhausted, worried, and in disbelief, I couldn't help but start to cry again and think of my mother, father, brothers, and family, how bad I wanted to hug them all, share my favorite meal, and listen to some merengue. I made one last round down in radio, and our systems were still down; we had no way to communicate besides our Iridium phone. The Iridium phone provides robust and secure voice connections around the world, and it has been used by the US Armed Forces and the US Government for over forty years. Our Commanding Officer was able to connect to our commanders above and provided information since the start of the attack.

My Chief was in radio and she said to go get some rest because it was going to be a long few days; she was so right about that. I headed to my berthing area and, thankfully, we had a bit of potable water, so I took a quick three-minute shower and brushed my teeth. I got into my rack and tried to get a few hours of sleep, but more was to come later that night. About two or three hours into my sleep, I heard shouting and screaming. I woke up and saw everyone getting dressed and screaming that water was coming into the berthing and we had to start doing damage control. I left the area because I was not part of the damage control team. I visited radio again just to see if anything was working, and to my frustration there was still no power to our equipment. I was still sleepy and tired, so I started asking where people were sleeping and I was told that most people were outside. So I took my blankets and laid them down on the hot and rough surface. It was definitely uncomfortable and superhot, but I did get a couple of hours of sleep before the sun was up by 5:00 a.m. and the temperature at over 90 degrees. As we started the second day, it was all about checking the different measurements of damage control on the ship, looking for food and water, and just trying to get a routine for however long we were going to be there.

Since the galley and the refrigerator decks were destroyed as well as all the food, all we had to eat was whatever food was stored on the ship store and the ship store storage. So we were eating Snickers bars with Gatorade or chips with soda— whatever we could find to keep us fed even if we had to do ration control. The Yemeni government tried to send us food from their fanciest hotel and restaurants, but we refused to eat it. We were on high alert; we didn't trust anybody, since we were the ones still standing watch both for damage control and also security 24/7. We had Sailors who manned the 50 Cal to defend against any water vessel attack, and others guarded the perimeter from the bridge of the ship. We only had each other as far as we were concerned; we didn't want anything from Yemen. Later that day, October 13, 2000, we received phones that could be used to make international calls. ITs like myself were tasked with keeping accountability of the phones and ensuring everyone could call home for three to five minutes on the first round.

This allowed each sailor to communicate to their family that they were ok. No matter how you felt, you were told to say that you were ok. The desire was to make our families worry less about the situation. It is one thing to be scared and another to be injured and still stuck in our situation. After two or three hours ensuring everyone made their initial phone call, it was my turn to call my mother. I had to look all over my coffin under my bed to find her number from the Dominican Republic since she had moved about two months prior. I found the number and rushed to the area where we could call and picked up a phone. By now it was the fourteenth of October, two days after the bombing. I dialed my mother, and her husband answered the phone. He was truly the last person I wanted to talk to, but he sounded concerned and said that my mom had not had any food or drink for over forty-eight hours. A few weeks earlier, she had received my pictures from Malta and in one of them you could see the number 67 on the side of the ship. In the videos that the news was showing, you could see almost the exact angle and that's how she was able to recognize it was my ship.

Because I didn't update my information, big Navy never contacted my mother. She got on the phone and I could hear her crying as well as praising God because she heard my voice. She asked if I was ok, and I responded "yes;" she asked if I was eating and sleeping ok, and I answered "yes." She continued to ask questions and my answers were very dry and to the point, a simple yes or no. Years later my mother would say that I sounded like a machine, that I was programmed to reply to her questions in a certain manner.

CHAPTER VII

It was so hot in Yemen that our Commanding Officer allowed us to relax our uniform. We could wear our coveralls halfway up and tie our sleeves to our waist and only wear the white T-shirt we usually wore under the coveralls. It was the third day after the bombing, October 15, 2000. We were doing a daily muster, which was the process or event of accounting for members in a military unit or ship. It was around 7:30 in the morning and the Chiefs directed us to put on our coveralls properly, even if it was 100 degrees already, because we were going to do colors. What are colors? Morning and evening colors refer to the raising and lowering of our national flag. Morning colors is the traditional flag-raising ceremony, which occurs every morning at 8:00 a.m. per US regulations, and evening colors is where we lower the flag during sunset. After colors were completed, I asked one of the Chiefs why we were doing colors while we were waiting for food, hot, and without clean water. He explained very firmly that it was our duty to restore order and tradition but, most importantly, that we needed to show them (those that attacked us) that "no matter what, this flag will fly" as he pointed to the Ensign. I will be honest and tell you that I didn't understand the importance of that statement at the time. I was too young and green to understand what it signified, both to whoever our adversary was and to our morale as Sailors in distress.

About an hour after that conversation, the Marines FAST team came to provide security onboard the ship and the surrounding area. The Fleet Anti-terrorism Security Team (FAST) platoons are an elite unit of the United States Marine Corps that is capable of rapidly deploying to immediately improve security at United States Government installations or situations worldwide. They are also capable of deploying as an infantry with quick reaction force. They took over the 50 Cals onboard, the bridge watches, and dropped armed boats. This allowed my shipmates to get more rest and finally eat right since we were getting food and water tested and safeguarded by the FAST team. Another few hours later, the USS *Camden* (AOE-2) arrived, who was a fast combat support ship, a type of replenishment auxiliary ship. Different from traditional logistic ships, the fast combat support ship is designed with high speed to keep up with the carrier battle group. The *Camden* and her crew provided hospitality services, and cleaned berthing and food for those who went onboard the ship. I was asked if I wanted to come to the ship and get a warm meal, a warm shower, and call my mother for a longer period of time. I and about ten others took a small boat to the *Camden*. As we climbed onboard, we noticed that part of the ship's crew was standing in two columns ready to salute us as part of an honor guard.

Once my foot hit the deck of the ship, I heard over the 1MC "heroes arriving," and everyone saluted me. I was so surprised and honored, I could only cry and smile at the same time because I was just touched that they did so much for us. I was taken to a stateroom, where I had my own private shower, queen bed, TV, and small fridge—the closest I would get to a cruise ship in the

Navy. I took the longest shower I have ever taken in my twenty years of life! I just wanted to feel water running over my body! After that I was able to eat in the wardroom, usually only for Officers, but I was allowed to eat there and order a la carte. I got the biggest steak they had, loaded potatoes, and chocolate ice cream. It was all delicious and a dream; my stomach hurt after because I had so much to eat. Then I went to their radio and I was able to talk to my mother again; this time, we talked for, like, forty-five minutes. I spoke with my mother, brother, and a couple of my aunts, and they even had time to get my father, who lived twenty minutes away, so I got to speak with him as well. We cried, laughed, and I felt encouraged that I would see them one day soon. I was drained, so I went to the stateroom and crashed. I think I slept anywhere between ten to twelve hours, hard yet comfortable sleep.-

Once I returned to the ship, I noticed that we had the Navy divers onboard to help rescue our brothers and sisters who were in the wreckage, underwater, or in other spaces we couldn't reach ourselves. We also noticed a horrible smell. We started questioning what that was, although we all kind of knew what it could be. The chain-of-command answer was rotten food, but we didn't have a lot of food in the refrigerator decks. It smelled like dead bodies and old blood, like death. As the Navy divers rescued one of my fallen shipmates, they were given the proper customs and traditions—body in casket, flag over it, six Sailors carried the casket, and honors passed over the 1MC. I was honored to volunteer to be one of the pallbearers for a good friend and IT. It was emotional but I had to show my respect for a friend.

Shortly afterward, I was asked by my Chief Petty Officer if I wanted to escort the body of my friend back to his family in the US. I thought about it; yes, I would get to go home sooner, but it was a huge responsibility to have to face a family and tell them that their loved one was dead. I said yes, and I left that evening. I looked for Rose and told her that I was leaving, that I was going to miss her, and that I looked forward to seeing her back in Virginia when the rest of the crew came back. I talked with my fellow ITs and thanked them for trusting me to represent the ship and escort one of us. I can't exactly remember how many of our shipmates we were escorting, but it was anywhere from seven to ten; each one had a personal escort as a sign of respect. They were part of the family and the family was never alone. We took a small boat from the FAST team and landed on the shores of Yemen, where the marines had set up a mini base. They had the perimeter fenced and plenty of marines guarded different areas inside the post and in the surrounding areas. We were treated to some US candy and drinks.

After about an hour of waiting, two trucks with large beds, where the caskets will be transported to the airport, showed up. The escorts followed in a bus with some marines, a translator from the embassy, and some local diplomats. We were all sitting in the bus when out of nowhere three or four marines started running to the bus and screaming to get out. Two of them took the driver out and had their guns drawn and pointed at him; the others took us back to the main building.

They explained that one of the trucks was suspected of having explosives since one of the service dogs walked around one truck no problem, and then as he was doing his round on the second truck, he just sat by one of the tires, which meant that he smelled something. I saw the marines take out the driver and ask him all kinds of questions, scream, yell, and even hit him over the head to get him to talk. They moved all the caskets to one truck, moved the suspected truck and driver to another location outside the perimeter, and we were escorted to the bus again. We started the drive to the airport, where a C-17 waited to take us all back to the US. A C-17 is a high-wing, four-engine, T-tailed military transport aircraft; the multi-service C-17 can carry large equipment, supplies, and troops directly to small airfields in harsh terrain anywhere in the world. On the way to the airport, we hit five or six checkpoints from the Yemeni police. Each time, they came onboard the bus and yelled while asking for our passports and military IDs. We were terrified since we didn't understand what they were saying and they were extremely aggressive. The translators did the best they could, but it was too many loud voices to not feel overwhelmed. We were told that the entire country was on high alert due to the amount of military personnel and equipment deployed by the Department of Defense due to the bombing of our ship. We got to the terminal and we were escorted to the flight line; the caskets were uploaded first and we waited on the side. Again, we had local police and military just looking at us while they carried their AK-47s. It just felt intimidating and unnecessary.

After about an hour, we boarded the plane, and right away we felt how cold it was. It was mostly a cargo ship and was also carrying caskets, so the AC was running high. We had uncomfortable seats, but we had each other. The flight was long, cold, and uncomfortable. Although, the crew had snacks and water for us, which was nice. Then, about five hours into the flight, the pilot came over the speakers and said that there was an issue in one of the engines, so we had to do an emergency landing at a base in Germany for repairs before we kept going to Delaware. My mind was just running, thinking what else could go wrong. Why so many hurdles and obstacles? We landed in Germany, no problem. The military terminal had restrooms, food, phones to call our family, and a small lounge where we could be more comfortable while we waited for the repairs and a change of crew. We had about a three-hour layover, and the plane was good to go. The next part of the journey was going to take another eight hours, so I bought another shirt to put on top of the one I had; I wanted more layers. We took off and we all found a space to lie down, even if it was on a metal platform. We just wanted to rest as much as possible before landing in Delaware since we didn't know what was expected of us. We landed in Delaware, and we were received by medics, military Officers, and some local politicians.

A Navy Admiral and an Army general spoke to us and told us how important it was that we did what we did, and how we honored our fallen brothers and sisters by bringing them home to their families. Then we were told that we would not escort our shipmates all the way to their perspective homes. The reason being they understood that we were not trained to do that. Our emotions would get the best of us and we would most likely show our emotions in front of the families, and that would probably hurt them even more. I was upset; I wanted to bring my friend to his family in Texas, tell his mother how amazing he was, and how much he helped me. But like any other sailor, I had to follow rules. We were told that we would take another short flight from Delaware to Norfolk, Virginia. I kept thinking: *This is how I'm going to spend my twentieth birthday, traveling across the world, exhausted mentally and emotionally?* We took three small private jets. I was on the first one scheduled to land in Norfolk. Once we landed in Norfolk, I stepped out and saw a lot of families, cameras from news channels, and more Navy officials.

A Navy chaplain embraced me and asked, "Where is your family?"

"They're not here; they're in Dominican Republic," I said.

"Well, your Navy family is here!" He gave me a big hug and took me inside.

There, we were told that we were going to get interviewed by FBI agents who had already started doing interviews back in Aden, Yemen onboard the ship and now wanted more details if we remembered anything new. Then we had to see a psychologist at the Portsmouth Hospital, and he had some generic questions that had scales from one to ten on how I felt, how angry or depressed I was, and others. Then he asked more personal questions, like how badly I wanted to see my mother, what was my motivation to stay alive, etc. We left the hospital in Portsmouth, Virginia and headed back to Norfolk to get some sleep in the nicest rooms they had on base. The next morning, I reported to an administration office, where I was asked to fill out some paperwork requesting a flight anywhere I wanted. Of course, I selected Dominican Republic to see my mother. Then I was told that the Navy was going to give me fourteen days of convalescent leave. I asked if I could add another seven days of my earned leave days, and they said yes. I called my mother, full of excitement since I was finally going to see her after all this time. She had one request: that I wear my dress uniform to the Dominican Republic. I was not too happy about that because I was flying on the twenty-first of October, which meant that I had to wear my dress blues to a tropical island. But after all she went through, I knew it was the least I could do.

I took the flight from Norfolk to Atlanta and then from Atlanta to Dominican Republic. On my second flight, one of the flight attendants saw that my unit identification code was from the USS *Cole* and she asked if I was part of the ship, and I said yes. About twenty minutes later, the head pilot came over the speakers and said, "We have a *Cole* hero onboard; please give a round of applause to him." It was so humbling and unexpected. Then I was told to move to first class and wait there after we landed because the pilots wanted to shake my hand. I had never been in first class, and back then it meant something—delicious food and drinks and world-class treatment. After a three-hour flight from Atlanta to Dominican Republic, we landed in Santo Domingo International Airport. I waited until everyone deplaned, and I talked to the pilots and took pictures. It was good to get to know people from another industry.

Once I cleared immigration and walked out, I saw my mother and she saw me. She ran to me and gave me the biggest hug; she didn't want to let me go, and I didn't either. We both cried and said that we loved each other at least five times. I was so relieved to see her and just hold her. We drove from the airport to my mother's house, a journey that took about forty minutes. We talked, sang along to the radio, and just talked about how happy I was to be home. Once at the house, at least 100 people were waiting for us—from family to close friends—and lots of food, drinks, and music. I put on more comfortable clothes and danced and ate with my folks; for a few hours, I forgot about the rest of the world.

The next day, I sat down and spoke with my mother about the entire experience on the *Cole*. I talked about the amount of death and pain I witnessed as well the acts of bravery performed by my shipmates. I was sad but also very proud of what we did as a team to save the ship and ourselves. My mother was very religious back then, so we had to go to a lot of churches and places because she made all kinds of promises if I made it back alive and well. Each day, we traveled to a different church or town, where either she or I had to do so many Hail Mary's or give some monetary donations. My mother's husband arranged a few interviews with news outlets and TV stations. I was not ready or happy to do that. Everything was extremely raw and hurtful to have to process and talk about, but I also wanted my nation to know the amazing sacrifices and heroism the crew showcased during the tragedy.

A few days before I had to head back to Norfolk, my mother's husband asked me if I could provide money for the bills and food. This request was shocking because my mother would have never asked me for that and also because they didn't need the money. My mother overheard and she was livid. She pulled him to the side and they argued, but I was already upset and just felt like shit. I gave him $400 and just went to my room. My mother came up and apologized. She was crying so I just hugged her and told her that I knew it was not her fault. I loved my mother so much and she always did and still does anything for me, so I knew she was deeply hurt. We moved on, and we enjoyed the last few days because I had to go back to work. We had one last big meal and, again, I was extremely grateful I had the opportunity to see my family again.

By the time I made it back to Norfolk, the rest of the crew was either back in Norfolk as well or on their way.

Most of them left after I did, and the final group left on November, 3, 2000. Once I went into the building where we had to muster, I saw a few of my brothers and sisters. It was so good to see them, talk to them, and hear that they were getting help just like I did. The first couple of days, we really didn't have much to do; we had to muster and then we were able to go back to our barracks and be off for the rest of the day. The base had just finished building brand-new barracks and we were sent there to live. I had my own room with a private door, and I shared the kitchen and bathroom. There were lounges with TVs and games, laundry rooms, and vending machines on each floor. Plus, the cable company gave us free cable for a year. It was a very nice room and environment.

After a few weeks, I was told that I could speak with my detailer (they're assigned to give you guidance and advice for your assignments/duty stations). I was told that I could pick anywhere I wanted to go as long as it was sea duty. So I asked to get a ship out of San Diego. I thought a single E-3 should be an easy transfer to another coast since ships always needed low-ranking Sailors and I didn't have a family, vehicle, or house of goods. I was sadly mistaken; the detailer said that they didn't have any billets for me in San Diego, so I had to pick a ship in Norfolk or stay with the *Cole*. I spoke with my chain of command, and they said that if I stayed with *Cole* I would be sent to a bunch of schools and would be able to be part of the ship coming back to life since it was going to be treated like a pre-commission unit. That was enough for me to be sold on the idea of staying. Plus I started talking with the girl from the ship again. She was heartbroken since the person that she dated for over two years on the ship was actually engaged to someone else. She only discovered it once the entire crew came back from Yemen, and the fiancée was waiting for him. She let me know that she didn't want to be with anybody, but I was persistent and was willing to bide my time.

In the meantime, I went to Navy schools and went out more since I obtained my license; yes, at twenty, almost twenty-one years old, and bought a used car for too much money and no real documentation on the car's history. I didn't know anything about getting a vehicle, but I saw a commercial that said "we will teach you how to drive and help you purchase a vehicle" from one of the local used-car dealers. They made it so convenient because they would even come to the base to pick me up, "help me" with finances, and get the license. They got me; it was a Dodge Plymouth that cost an even 10k. I don't remember the year, and it was dark green. It looked clean and in great condition. I got my license and I just signed whatever they put in front of me. This car would let me see my mom instead of taking the Greyhound bus, allow me to get whatever food I wanted without having to rely on others, and let me hit the clubs and bars without having to ask others for rides. At work, we were told that we were going to move to Pascagoula, Mississippi since that's where the ship would be fixed. While a lot was happening in my life, I moved to Mississippi with the rest of the ship crew. We moved into a barracks and had to work in the ship yard as the ship was coming back to life. After a few weeks down there, a few things became clear. One, I was in the south! I was too dark for some parts of town and I was too light for other parts of town. Second, due to some valid threats, we were on higher alert while rebuilding the ship, which meant more personnel provided armed watches, and that meant we needed more personnel for duty day. So our duty days went from every six days to every three days. Three days, we were there to work—to get the ship back to the fight and show the world the USS *Cole* would never be defeated.

Around December of 2000, the NFL asked the Navy to provide some Sailors to do the color guard for the Super Bowl since it would be in the Superdome (as it was called back then) in New Orleans.

The chain of command decided that they would break down the five positions needed for the color in pay grades. One E-3 and below, one E-4, one E-5, one E-6, and one E-7 and above. All the Officers and Chiefs voted on who would represent each pay grade and lucky enough, I was selected as the E-3 and below sailor. I couldn't believe it; I was so excited and nervous because I knew it was a lot of responsibility, but I looked forward to it. For the next six weeks, we drove from Pascagoula, Mississippi to New Orleans, Louisiana, and practiced drill, marching steps, and all the necessary customs and courtesies to do colors for an event like that. The first couple of sessions, we were horrible; we practiced for three to four hours. The practices were in the middle of the field, in the sun, but it was better than standing duty almost every other day. It was our escape for a few days each week. Since we were in New Orleans, we took advantage of the proximity to Bourbon Street. Wow, what a time and how many crazy things we said and even experienced. We told the girls to hold on to the loops in our pants so they wouldn't get lost in the crowd. The amount of breasts I saw from the balconies and just because was insane—people had sex in the side streets, used the streets as bathrooms, and much more.

CHAPTER VIII

The Super Bowl weekend was finally here. It was February of 2001. During the rehearsal on Friday and Saturday, we practiced with some of the artists that were performing. Mariah Carey sang the national anthem, and Mary J. Blige with Mark Anthony sang "America the Beautiful." After one of the practices, we all met Mariah Carey and I even gave her hug. I held her for so long that her bodyguard tapped me on the shoulder and said, "Bro, that's enough." She was a good sport since she only smiled and left. We talked to the Rams cheerleaders and were invited to the *Maxim* magazine party, but I was too scared to attend since I was under twenty-one; what a shame! We did a great job during the Super Bowl and were invited to stay on the field for the remainder of the game, but our Commanding Officer said that we had tickets somewhere else and we had to sit there; another missed opportunity during that weekend. The game was awesome and we had a great time even though we had to wear our uniforms the entire time. A few weeks after the Super Bowl, we started moving onboard the ship. Work and sleep on the ship was a challenge. I started having nightmares, anxiety, and depression. I was told to see a counselor and fill out some paperwork, and it was determined that I had to leave the ship and head back to Norfolk. I was placed on limited duty, which meant that I couldn't be onboard ships until I saw a psychologist and I was properly diagnosed and treated. I was happy heading back to Norfolk since the girl I liked was there along with most of the people I knew.

My best friend from high school was also stationed in Norfolk, so we figured out a way to get into clubs since we were not over twenty-one. Back then our military ID was laminated, so we printed the back of an ID that had a date of birth that would put us over twenty-one and relaminated the ID so we were both twenty-two. We were able to get away with those things within the military because they only checked the front to see if the picture and name matched; so we got into clubs and got alcohol with no problem. The next thing was finding Spanish clubs or at least ones that had Latin nights. In our quest, we found a great lineup that started on Wednesday with salsa night at the base club, Thursday was Latin nights at The Alley, Friday was Elegant, Saturday back to The Alley, and Sunday it was Knickerbockers. We went each night for weeks or skipped one night or another, but on average it was three nights per week of clubbing. I met some amazing people, danced for hours, and expanded my experiences with women. I met women my age, older, or much older, like forty or forty-five years old. We had some great times, wild times, and scary times. My friend used his ID so much, in and out of his wallet, that one of the corners was coming off. So when he gave it to a bouncer, the bouncer peeled the corner and saw that it was a fake. He stopped my best friend and called the base security and turned him over to them. He was ordered by his chain of command to do a presentation about disobedience—an order that got us to stop doing that dumb stuff.

In another area of my life, I was trying my best to get with Rose, the girl I liked from the ship. We kind of started to date seriously after me almost begging; I say almost begging because I asked her out like four or five times and she was very reluctant to say yes. Rose was very honest about how she felt, that she still had feelings for that old boyfriend who lied to her about having a fiancée. We saw each other here and there and hooked up, but she was never really into me like I was into her. For Valentine's Day, I sent her some flowers and a teddy bear since I was in Mississippi with part of the crew while the ship was getting fixed. I didn't get an email or phone call saying anything from her. So after I left work, I called her. It was about 8:00 p.m., and I asked her if she received my gifts and she said yes. I was hurt that all day had passed, yet I didn't get a "got it" or "thank you" or whatever. This was after she humiliated me after the command Christmas party. I got us a beautiful room on the Virginia Beach strip. The room had a big balcony with an amazing view of the ocean, a huge jetted hot tub, and a second separate room for our friends. Well, after the party was over she wanted to go dancing at a club on the strip, and I just wanted to stay in the room. I told her to go with her friends and I would wait for her at the room. Around 2:00 a.m. Rose showed up with six or seven friends, which was bad enough, but the humiliation came when I saw the last person in the group, the guy that had broken her heart. She invited him to our room, he made eye contact with me as he was coming in and asked her, "Hey, whose room is this?" She said my name and, thankfully, he left, but I was already hurt. Yet I continued to date her and just continued to put myself last.

It was a tough lesson, but we continued, and when things were right it was lovely. Rose and I decided to break up due to the distance, and since we were not in the best place anyways. But, of course, we didn't take the necessary precautions a couple having sex should. She discovered that she was pregnant a few months later. I was shocked when she told me, but also extremely happy. Being a dad sounded amazing, especially having a beautiful baby with Rose. She was not as excited as I was and mentioned a few times that she might not even keep the baby. Rose returned from Mississippi, she was there before me. I excitedly picked her up from the airport since I was over the moon about becoming a dad and hopefully us being together. After a cold hug at the airport and very small conversation on the ride to her house, she looked at me before she stepped out of the car and said, "Don't think because I'm pregnant that we will be together." Another blow to my heart, pride, and desires. In that very moment, I said enough. I hoped she would keep the baby, but I was ok not having a romantic relationship with her.

While all that was happening, she complained to a doctor about having pain during sex with me. The doctor told her to tell me to see him so I could get checked. I was so young and naïve that I did. He asked me to drop my pants so he could examine my penis, and he started to suck on it. I completely froze and immediately felt scared and ashamed of myself. I will expand more later because right now it will derail my thoughts and my story.

Right around the same time I found out that I was going to have a baby and Rose didn't want to be with me, I started to play the field. I met different women in different places, like the clubs I was visiting, on base, or even at the mall. I was enjoying life and finding a way to feel wanted after I was turned down again and again by the same lady. One girl, who was a dental technician in the Navy, let's call her Lola, took interest in me and we started hooking up. One day while having sex, the condom broke and neither of us realized it until I had finished in her. A few weeks later, Lola showed me her results of a pregnancy test; it was positive! Now I had two women pregnant within weeks apart; I was not happy. I told Lola that I didn't want her to have the baby and that I already had one coming, and the only reason she was pregnant was because the condom broke. She didn't want to give the baby up but I kept insisting. I would go as far as to say, "If you keep it, that baby is only going to see my paycheck, because I don't want anything to do with it."

A few weeks later, as I was walking into the building and a bunch of people were in the lobby, Lola followed me and gave me a note from the doctor with the date and time of her abortion, plus the next test saying she was not pregnant. I didn't know what to say so I just said thank you. She started yelling, "Baby killer" and "there goes the baby killer" until I got in the elevator. She did that a few more times until she eventually stopped. I felt horrible, but I won't lie, I also felt relieved. For the first couple of weeks of the pregnancy Rose was not sure if she wanted to keep it, so I was nervous and sad. But I always believed it was a woman's body, so she had the right to do what she believed was best. I asked myself why I was ok with Rose having a baby but not Lola. I kept coming back to the fact that I actually was in love with Rose. I was hoping we would be together in the future. I also felt this sense of anger because Lola didn't understand that I didn't want a baby with her, which is why I wore a condom; it just happened to break during sex. One day Rose spoke with one of those ladies that read cards to tell the future, and she said, "The best thing in your life is in your belly." Thankfully, that was enough for her to keep the baby. She was still upset that she was pregnant and for some reason blamed me. I say for some reason since we both were not using any kind of protection, and even using the pulling out method was never going to be a good idea. Her dislike was so bad that she didn't want to see me at all. I just wanted to talk to the belly so my child could hear my voice.

Thankfully, her mom moved in with her and she would let me in the house and make Rose just sit there so I could read to the belly. Around my birthday in October 2001, I received a call and she said, "Are you ready to be a dad of a girl?" I was lost for words. I always thought that I wanted a boy as my first child, but once she said that, all I could think was how much I was going to love her and protect her. I was in heaven. We talked about what name to use and she said that she always liked Belén, which is "Bethlehem" in Spanish. I bought a year's supply of diapers, clothes, shoes, things a baby would need, and anything she needed and I could afford. I was so happy to be a father, and I wanted to show her that she had nothing to worry about as far as me being responsible. I met someone else within a few months of the pregnancy in one of the Latin clubs. That relationship would change my life in my ways and not all good.

The new girl I was dating was very sexy, loved to dance, have fun, and was also in the Navy. We got close very quickly, and after only a few months of dating we moved in together. It sounded like a good decision, mostly because I didn't want to live in the barracks anymore (which, looking back, that was dumb because I had all I needed in the barracks), and we wanted to come home to the same space. The only problem was that my Navy salary was super low and I was not getting the housing allowance that started after you became an E-5. This meant that I paid for half of rent, car payment, a high insurance premium since I was a young driver, cell phone bill, half of the bills on the house, gas, etc. Soon I was paying for basic things like groceries or gas with credit cards because I couldn't afford it out of my regular paycheck.

Once we moved in together, we both encountered issues that I'm sure most young lovers encounter—lots of jealousy and controlling behavior. She told me not to go to Jersey to see my mother, not because she didn't want to see my mother, but because she wanted to spend more time with me. I wouldn't make things easier for her, because I was a flirt and had the tendency to hook up with women as soon as we would have one of our many break ups. I also had controlling inclinations that contributed to her behavior instead of owning that I was just as controlling and jealous as she was.

CHAPTER IX

Now it's January 2002. Rose was almost due and I worked shift schedule. I got a message from her that she was in the hospital and going to deliver within a few hours. I can't recall why I couldn't be there but I was not there for the delivery, and I didn't get to see my daughter until the next day. My little angel was born January 18, 2002, and when I saw her the next day, she melted in my arms. I was in love right away. She was so beautiful and peaceful. Her mom said, "Tickle her cheeks," so I did and to my surprise she smiled and she had dimples just like me. Talk about seeing your image and seeing my mother's image since I looked like her, and my daughter now looked like her too. I held her for a while and gave her kisses and changed her once. I left about two or three hours later, and once I got in the car with my girlfriend she said, "I don't want you to see her without me." I said, "Well, her mom doesn't like you, so what am I supposed to do?" And she said figure it out, but you don't need to be there with just her. It sounded unreasonable and just cruel, yet my young and stupid self complied. I didn't see my daughter again until about a week later.

I will make something clear before I continue to talk about my relationship with my girlfriend at the time. She asked and even demanded some unbelievable things, but I still had to do them. She didn't have a gun to my head or abuse me physically to do it. I did it, and I have to take full responsibility for putting our relationship above my child, my mother, and my friends. We had many arguments about different things, like when I called the mother of my child and said, "How are you doing?" In my girlfriend's eyes, there was no need for that. I just needed to ask about the baby and talk about when I was going to pick her up, etc. Some of the fights turned into ugly events. I grabbed her to stop her from hitting me or she threw my clothes in the street, only for one of us to beg the other to get back together. This unhealthy relationship continued for over two years, with lots of cheating and hurtful behaviors. Yet I still proposed and spent thousands of dollars that I didn't have on the best ring I could find, with diamonds and white gold. During all of that, I was still going to see a psychologist, since I was diagnosed with Post-traumatic stress disorder (PTSD), which is a disorder that develops in some people who have experienced a shocking, scary, or dangerous event. After nine months of limited duty, I was cleared for sea duty again. Yes, I still had my PTSD, but I was considered well enough to rejoin the fleet.

During that time in limited duty, I didn't take care of myself very well, mostly not working out or doing things I enjoyed. So I learned a big lesson that would stay with me for the rest of my military career. Once I was clear, I was required to take my physical fitness assessment (PFA) since I didn't have a physical injury. Well, I hadn't exercised in months. I was super nervous the day of, and I had two bananas and lots of water about thirty minutes before the test. I did my required amount of curl-ups, which was eighty or above within two minutes, then my required amount of pushups, which was seventy or above within two minutes. Now it was time for the run. I was super nervous and already tired from the other two events. I started well, but soon enough I was running out of gas and my stomach hurt. About a mile into it, I threw up for, like, thirty or forty-five seconds. I was told to continue running the other half of the mile since I was doing good on time. Well, when I crossed the finish line, I was told that I failed by twelve seconds. This meant that I had to be enrolled in the fitness enhancement program (FEP). It was so embarrassing since I was a 5'11" 159 lb. young man that had no business in FEP. To make things worse, a month later I was selected for E-5, but I couldn't be officially promoted until I passed my PFA. It was the worst month mentally for me since the bombing. I buckled down and passed the PFA a month later, in November of 2002, and I was promoted to E-5.

It was 2003 now, and I and my girlfriend were both scheduled to make a deployment in early 2004, but in separate aircraft carriers, me on the USS *George Washington* and her on the USS *Enterprise*. That year, we did a lot of exercises in preparation for the deployment, which meant that we both would be underway at sea a lot, which only added to the jealousy and issues we had. She mentioned that she would try to swap with another sailor so she could come to my ship and do the deployment with me. I always thought that it was just talk. My daughter was sixteen or eighteen months old, and I saw her more often even if my girlfriend tried to find excuses as to why I shouldn't pick her up. It was always something about us not spending enough time together, which was not true, but it was her way to have me all to herself. In mid-October of 2003, I took her home to New Jersey so she could meet my mother, who had gotten divorced and moved back to New Jersey after she sold the house and sold her half of the business she had with her partner because he wanted cash as part of the divorce. She was devastated and went back to her old job in Queens, New York to make a living again. I wanted to see her before my fiancée and I took a trip to the Dominican Republic so she could meet my father and the rest of my family. While in New Jersey, she dressed very provocatively and even inappropriately. My mom asked why she could see her ass cheeks in her jeans, with holes right under her ass, or why she wore a top that was see-through or too short. But the most insulting thing to my mother was her demanding I get Chinese food for her instead of eating my mother's food. All that, together with my mother knowing all the things we had struggled with, made her not a favorite. We left that Sunday after four days in Jersey and I just felt embarrassed, but that was just the start of the bad impression on my family.

Our trip to DR started great. I booked a hotel right by the harbor in the capital, Santo Domingo, mostly because I always dreamed of staying there when I was super poor. We landed and everything was going beautifully; the hotel room was amazing as well as the pool on the rooftop. The hotel was hosting the Brazilian soccer team, and I was mistaken for one of the players a few times, so I received extra-nice treatment by the staff and people around the hotel. We went to my grandparents' house, where my dad and other family members lived. He was so impressed, not happy, but impressed by how good looking and sexy (his words) she was. To ensure he was not the only one that felt that way, he took her to the corner store, where a bunch of his friends and guys my age were playing dominoes and drinking while merengue was playing on the loud speakers. My dad danced with her and she could really dance, so he enjoyed it too much and stopped her at the point where her ass faced the crowd and he asked the men what they thought.

Yup, you read that right, my dad showcased my fiancée, who loved the attention as well. I was still talking to my aunts and cousins, so I was a few minutes behind to the spectacle, but when I finally saw what was happening, I had to be held back by my family because I wanted to fight my father. The rest of the trip was argument on top of argument, from her not liking me greeting my cousins with a kiss on the cheeks to me getting mad because men would look at her, as she wore sexy clothes. We made it back and then it was time to do what we call work-ups exercises. These were underway periods that we did to ensure all our systems worked properly. We did testing so that the strike group, aircraft carrier, and other ships could work as one. During one of the exercises, we lost a plane that was not able to land on the carrier by hooking the tailhook to the arresting wire on the aircraft carrier. The pilot was not able to eject from his seat on time and he lost his life. I had so many flashbacks due to the big alarm sounds and the announcement of lost lives. We lost another sailor because he walked in front the turbine and was sucked in. It was a tough couple of weeks, but thankfully, as soon as we came back to land, I made an appointment to see a psychologist and talk about my flashbacks and feelings.

Now it's January 2004, and it was time for me to go on deployment. My girlfriend was already on hers. The deployment was very stressful. Between having one of the two supervisor positions and standing watch for twelve hours daily, I was always tired and held responsible for anything that had to do with communications or networks within the strike group. I either should have known what was going on in other ships or I should have had a solution for their issues. Every day, I briefed a two-star admiral, and I felt the immense pressure every single time. With time, I got better during my brief by preparing myself on the things I expected to be asked. I had great advice from my division officer, a Lieutenant Commander, who said, "You're the subject-matter expert; the admiral has another 1000 things to worry about, if you sound confident about your report and answers, he will start to ask less and just trust you." I really needed to hear that, and just like that, she said the briefs got a lot easier as I became more confident.

Deployment was all about routines. You woke up at the same time, ate at the same time and sat at the same area, worked out at the same time, and just followed the routine until you hit a port or the ship had a change of schedule or daily routine. Even the menu onboard the ship was the same Monday through Sunday. It might sound crazy to most people, but having a set schedule and menu took away a level of stress. You knew what you were eating Tuesday, tacos; you knew what you were eating Saturday, pizza and wings; it just took away the thinking aspect of what am I eating today? Doesn't sound like much, but it was all about routines.

We visited Souda Bay, Greece as our first port. It was a very nice island that provided lots of amazing food and shops. From there, we set sail to the Middle East, where we had an extra dose of Dubai. Dubai was beautiful but also expensive and hot. I was able to talk to my daughter and my mother often while underway and when we pulled in to these ports. My daughter was only two, so I got a couple of sentences in before she dropped the phone or passed it to her mom. I also communicated with my fiancée at the time. She was enjoying her deployment as well and made the impossible happen. She was able to find a person on my carrier who had the same career field, the same amount of time left on the command, and the same Navy schools as her, and she was going to swap with this person and be on my deployment. For the other sailor, it was an easy decision—leave the current ship, who still had four months left of deployment, and go to another ship that was finishing its deployment and then was going into major repairs, which meant the ship would not go underway for years.

For my Fiancée, it meant that she would be on deployment for close to ten months. She didn't mind since it meant she would be with me and also make extra money because all Sailors made extra money out to sea since we received a few incentives, and sailing in the Middle East meant tax-free income. She was flown into the ship a few weeks before we left the Middle East, and right away there were issues between us. She accused me of doing something with any girl that said hi to me in front of her, and in no time I was acting the same way. They always say that working together is a bad idea; well, I found out the hard way.

We hit our next port, Naples, Italy. It was ok, but too dirty, and she only wanted to stay in the hotel, which, of course, we did. After seven long months, late in 2004, we finally made it home, but by then the relationship was at its worst. She still didn't want me to see my daughter as often as I wanted, the jealousy was crazy, and we still found ways to see other people by breaking up for a few days and then getting back together.

Finally, one episode of rage forced me to move on for good. We had broken up, to the point that I moved to my own place. Like every other time, we got back together, but I said we should stay living in our own places for a while to see if it would work this time. A couple weeks later, I purchased a used computer from a friend of mine. I didn't know it had saved porn and porn sites on its browser history. That day, she wanted to see me and I said ok, but I had to hit the gym for about an hour. I left a key under the welcome mat. I went to the gym and worked out for a little over an hour. Back then your phone didn't have music, so I left it in the car and didn't see it again until after. I saw that I had fifty-six missed calls and about fifteen voice messages. She was angry that she found porn on the computer. In her mind, I was watching porn and that was cheating. Since I didn't answer, each message sounded angrier and crazier. By the time I listened to message eight or nine, I heard her throwing my stuff around the house and just breaking things.

Once I made it to my apartment, I saw dishes on the floor, my PlayStation inside of the wall since she threw it so hard, and clothes all over the place. She saw me and rushed to me and started hitting me on my chest and arms. I will admit I didn't descale the situation, since after she kept asking if I watched the porn, I said yes just to make her angrier. It was a dumb move but I was tired of her being angry for no reason, so in my eyes I was going to give her a real reason to be angry. I guess I took the saying "I will give you something to cry about" to heart. I finally got tired of yelling, getting hit, and seeing my things get destroyed, so I called the cops. They advised me to lock myself in a room. I couldn't understand, since she was the one acting crazy and breaking my stuff, but they just wanted us to be separated until the cops arrived. I managed to get into my room and lock the door while she continued to scream and throw things. Then all of a sudden it was quiet. I called 911 again and asked for a status on the police, and the operator said five more minutes. Out of the blue, I heard two slaps back-to-back. At first, I didn't know if it was her hitting something or herself. When the cops arrived, she met them first and said that I had hit her and slapped her a couple of times.

Thankfully, one of the Officers was a twenty-plus year veteran and he asked to see my hands and said, "Those are not his prints," then he turned to me and said, "Is this your apartment? Does she live here? If not, you can press charges." I said "No, I just want her out of my house and I can give her the jacket, pair of shoes, and toothbrush she has here." I did just that and they escorted her out.

I called my LPO at the time, who became my close friend during deployment, and told him what happened. He said very firmly, "You will change your cell number and not tell her. If I find out that she has your new number, I will report you to the Commanding Officer for not obeying an order." I found out years later that he couldn't demand that, let alone me get in trouble for not doing it, but honestly it was what I needed. I truly don't know if I would have stopped talking to her and eventually get back together. Later that evening, I called my mother crying. Crying because I let it get that far, crying because I still wanted to make it work and just feeling sorry for myself. She told me that today it was me that she was putting her hands on, but tomorrow it could be her granddaughter, and that she knew that I would have hurt her if she touched my baby girl. So she begged me to stop seeing her. I listened to my mother, and the next few months if she emailed me or called me at work, I ignored the emails and calls. My LPO told everyone that if she called asking for me, that the call should be put on speaker or forwarded to him. She had this fake New York accent since she was from Texas, so her voice was easy to recognize. Since she was also Navy, my LPO could ask her what she wanted with me. He would say to her, "Since the call is professional, you can tell me or say it on speaker phone." All that help, but my young heart still missed her and I wondered about her, so I made the decision that I needed to take orders overseas to get away.

I was not strong enough to be in the area even with my beautiful princess there. I just couldn't control my feelings. I spoke with my counselor and she said, "Are you sure that leaving your daughter and support system is the best thing?" I said, "Ma'am, I don't know, but I don't want to fall back to that horrible relationship." The next week, I applied for order and in February of 2005, I was selected for orders to Bahrain. I was happy and sad at the same time. Sad because I was not strong enough, and now I was going to be away from my daughter and mother. Around that time is when I started to use Myspace a lot more, and one day I saw this beautiful lady who caught my attention. She was from Brazil and worked at BET. We messaged each other and decided to meet for dinner in New York City. I was shocked. She was beautiful in her pictures but in person it was another level. She was almost six feet tall, beautiful tan skin, long black hair, and hazel eyes, small waist but big hips and booty, thick legs, and just elegant and beautiful. We talked and laughed and just enjoyed each other's company. A couple of dates later, and we were dating. It was challenging since she lived and worked in New York City and I lived in Norfolk, Virginia, but we made every effort to see each other. Things became more complicated when I was sent to a Navy school in Augusta, Georgia.

I was going to be in school for almost three months, and driving to New York was going to be out of the question, so we talked on the phone a lot. We discussed the future and just what was next for both of us, but I quickly learned how much she let her parents influence her decision-making. She was thirty and still asked permission to do certain things, like travel outside the state, make big purchases, and even getting a tattoo. I was done with school in Augusta, so I was able to take up to thirty days of leave before heading to Bahrain and my next duty station. I made plans with my Brazilian girlfriend so I could meet her parents and spend as much time as possible in New York together before

I spent my last week with my daughter. Well, as we were having dinner with her parents, she sat on her dad's lap for a while. I don't know what it was about it that just didn't feel right; maybe it was the fact that she was thirty years old or the way he rubbed her back and legs, it was a weird dynamic. I returned to Virginia and spent time with my baby girl. She was now four and super smart. I felt guilty that I was so weak that I needed to move overseas to get over someone. She didn't deserve for her dad to be gone, she didn't deserve to have less pictures and memories of us during those years, and she didn't deserve that I put my needs ahead of hers.

In the early months of 2006, I landed in Bahrain for the first time. I was shocked how hot it was, even though we landed at 2:00 a.m. Going through the process of checking in to a new base is always a pain, and it only gets worse when the base is overseas and you add the different culture, customs, and language. Thankfully, in Bahrain English was the main language spoken since it used to be an English colony. Within a couple of months, I was able to get an apartment out in town. Military members paid so much more than locals in rent that I was able to negotiate a fully furnished apartment, which is common there, but I wanted everything brand new. I wanted TVs, an AC, plus ceiling fans in all the rooms, and I wanted cable from four different countries. I also asked for a new George Foreman grill since they had just come out. To my surprise, I got all that and even a maid who cleaned twice a week and a rental car once a month for weekends since I didn't bring a vehicle. To this day, it was the most luxury and comfort I have ever had. Work was shift work, with enough days off to sleep since I worked mostly nights, and also time off to enjoy the island. There were a lot of rules we had to obey, like having curfews and not drinking in certain places, but there were a lot of clubs, restaurants, and women from all over Africa and Asia.

I quickly got the hang of my job and responsibilities and undertook a few collateral duties and just stayed out of the way and did what I was told. Honestly, I was not too focused on my career, although right before I reported to Bahrain, I had re-enlisted for six years. As expected, the Brazilian lady and I ended it after only a couple of months of me getting to Bahrain. The calls became less frequent and we couldn't agree on important things moving forward, like future locations and babies. It also didn't help that she got into it with my mother because she came to visit and provided my brother alcohol although he was a minor. No hard feelings between us, but she was very upset that we couldn't make it work. For me it was rational, and as a twenty-five-year-old man, I was ready to enjoy "my freedom."

One of the biggest things for guys in the island was hooking up with air crew or air attendants from Air India. Not only were the ladies beautiful and from all over the place, but they also all stayed in this one building, about five floors with six apartments per floor and each apartment would have at least one lady. I can tell you this is true: I met one lady at an Irish pub and she took me home. The next morning as I was walking out, another lady from another apartment asked me for my number, and we hooked up the next time she was in town. By the time I left

Bahrain fourteen months later, I had hooked up with six or seven ladies who worked for Air India. I only went home twice while in Bahrain, which means that I only saw my daughter twice in that amount of time. I didn't think of it much. I guess I understood that I couldn't afford a trip more often or that I didn't have the leave days to do that. Admittedly, I was too focused on me and the fun I was having. It's hard to come to grips with that reality. I don't know if I was a bad dad, but I was definitely not a great dad. The time came to pick my next assignment, and once again my focus was me and what I needed. The Navy was offering extra money to go to certain places in Europe, so to me it was a no-brainer. I joined so I could travel, and I was going to get extra money to live in the places I dreamed about? Sign me up! It was between Naples, Italy or England. The extra money was a lot higher for Naples compared to England, but I was told Naples was rough living and work was not the best.

I was selected for orders to England with a three-month Navy school en route. Thankfully, the school was in Virginia. My daughter's mom was deployed, and since I was going to be staying in a hotel for three months, she said I could stay in her room so I could see my daughter daily and just make my daughter's grandma feel safer with a man in the house. It was so good to spend time with my princess, teach her things, take her out, and help grandma. I bought a brand-new white G37 Infinity with tinted windows and black rings to take to England, and I visited my mother a few times in New Jersey during the three months of my school. The time came to ship my car and get prepared to fly to England. It was winter of 2007. I was told by my sponsor in England that it was going to be cold and rainy, but she coordinated for a taxi to pick me up and drive me to the base, which was eighty miles away from Heathrow Airport. It was an overnight commercial flight, so I landed around 6:00 a.m. and the taxi driver was waiting for me with a sign as soon as I stepped out of immigration. We started the drive to Royal Air Force Alconbury, or more simply RAF Alconbury; it was raining the entire drive and it was cold as advertised.

Once on base, my sponsor was waiting for me and had my room reserved with some water, food, and snacks, which was a really nice touch. The first three weeks were all about understanding my job and responsibilities, doing the base indoctrination, and finding a place to live. During indoctrination, we were told that we should understand that England could be very cold and gloomy due to all the rain and the short amount of sunlight. Most days, the sun didn't come up until 8:00 a.m. and it was dark by 4:00 or 4:30 p.m., and since I had to be at work at 7:00 a.m. and out by 4:00 p.m. in a building without windows, I felt like I was always in the dark. They recommended that we should have some lamps with high LED lights that would simulate sunlight inside the house, but I said no because I just felt like I would be ok. I found a very nice house at a village close by, and my car arrived about a month after my arrival.

When I checked in to medical and dental, I had to turn in my records; back then it was all on paper. During my check in process, I met this beautiful lady. She had a US Air Force uniform on but had a British accent, which I loved. I asked her how was that possible. She smiled since I was not the first person who asked her that, and she told me that her mother was British and that she was born in the town next to the base, and that her mom married an American and they moved to the US years ago. During that period, she became a citizen of the United States and enlisted in the Air Force years later. I saw her a few days later at the gym with her boyfriend so I knew she was not going to pay me any mind. But I was wrong, because later on I saw her again. This time, she was on her own and I was ready to make my move.

For the next four months or so, I noticed that I was always tired and feeling sluggish. Then I was feeling depressed, so I made an appointment to talk to a counselor and just ensure my PTSD was not making me feel this way. First, my counselor was an older British lady and she was awesome. She was very blond and cursed a lot, because she would be to the point. Second, she said I definitely needed those lights for my apartment, and, lastly, she told me to get a routine down that included working out and seeing the country and Europe. My counselor said something on our second session that has stuck with me to this day. She said, "I want you to think about an alcoholic or drug addict who is clean; they always know how many days they have been clean. Do you know why? It's because they know any day they can go back on that path. So think of that as far as your PTSD; it's something that will always be a part of you, and some days it will be perfectly fine, but others you will fall into that dark path. So you have to continue to take care of yourself and seek help often enough." Those words stayed with me forever and truly helped me understand how my PTSD affected me.

This duty station was the first time Chief Petty Officers really talked to me about my career. Yes, I had others that saw potential or even set me up for success, like when I was attached to carrier strike group eight and I won Junior Sailor of the year as an E-5. In England, I was held accountable for my bad study habits, and how that was the only thing that stopped me from getting a promotion since I was already maxed out in all the other areas, like award points, evaluation points, and time in rate points. Up to that point, I took my advancement exam for E-6 a total of five times. The exam happened twice a year, so Sailors had the opportunity to advance if they were eligible to take the exam for the next pay grade. My Chief made me enroll in a class after working hours, where Petty Officer First Class taught basic military requirements, which was 40–45 percent of our exam. My scores drastically improved, and I finally advanced to the E-6 pay grade. With that, my attitude and desire to continue to move up the ranks just increased significantly.

I had a sit-down with one of my Chiefs and I asked him what I needed to do to get a higher evaluation mark, even after only a year as a Petty Officer First Class. He said to be a subject matter expert or SME in my job and duties, and take care of the Sailors under my department, meaning that I had to ensure I was a voice for my Sailors, a supportive yet demanding leader who wanted them to maximize their potential. Lastly, to contribute to the command by taking on collateral duties that would enhance the mission by keeping training relevant, readiness up to date, and high standards. I also spoke with my division officer since I didn't have a Chief in my department, and I asked her what her expectations were. This would help me understand what she felt was important and how she dealt with different situations. I also provided my expectations to her after I had a couple of days to digest hers.

CHAPTER X

After six months living in England, I finally started to venture out to different cities around the UK. I drove to London, Birmingham, Cardiff, Bath, Oxford, Swansea, Reading, and a few more. Work was going great. I was exploring the country and I was talking to my daughter and mother regularly, but my demons were there manifesting in different ways. Of course, back then I didn't think there was anything wrong with disliking my father or should I say holding so many grudges for him. No matter what he did, holding grudges only consumes you since you're the one who thinks about it all the time; you're the one that gets angry or sad; and you're the only one that can let those feelings affect other things in your life. I would not talk to him, and my mother almost begged me to contact him, and even when I did, I was upset and irritated with him. The crazy part is that because of my mother's request and reasoning, I again started working on his visa application to live in the US, a process I started back in 2007 while in Bahrain.

I knew it was going to take some time because of all the paperwork that was required as well as the money that it took to get things done. Now in England, the process was still happening and I was constantly having to stay on top of him to take care of the different documents, blood work, and exams. So I was dealing with that for months, which only added to my dislike for him. But I knew that as my dad, I owed him the opportunity to have a better life in the US.

Another demon, or just bad habit, was being a womanizer. For one reason or another, I was having a lot of success approaching ladies and getting them to go out with me. Nothing wrong with that, but I was not being honest with the ladies I was seeing. I was seeing multiple women at the same time without them knowing or, at the very least, me mentioning. One worked on one base, another in the other base, one by my village, and the other two a little further out. Yes, at one point I was sleeping with five and sometimes six women at once. It got to the point where I had it lined up one per day. Lady Elena I saw on Mondays; lady Camila I saw on Tuesdays; lady Liliana I saw on Wednesdays, etc. It was just disrespectful in so many ways. I could have given these ladies a STD or infection or anything else. I really didn't care; I was just worried about what I wanted and what I was getting out of each relationship. The craziest part was since I was only seeing most of them once or maybe twice a week, they wanted to enjoy our time together to the maximum; they wanted dinner with a movie or show and to be intimate for hours.

It got to the point that I had to take leave and lie to most of them about me going out of town, all because I simply wanted to take a break, yet this continued to happen for months. If one got tired of dealing with the lack of affection or time together, then I would find someone to take that day. If it sounds shameful and even disgusting, it's because it was. Yet at the time, I didn't think anything bad about it. I didn't care about their feelings; my only true concern was to get caught and that person telling the others. It was a mess that I kept going for a while, but I was still doing great at work and being active with my family and friends. One day at work, an email was sent out requesting an E-6 with a specific clearance level, which I had, to head on temporary additional duty, or TAD, to the Netherlands. I jumped at the opportunity and I was selected. I was authorized to drive from England to Netherlands, get a furnished apartment, and I would receive extra money via per diem. On the drive, I stopped in France, Belgium, and Germany. I stopped in the best cities and had some amazing food. I arrived in Netherlands and was quickly introduced to the team that I was going to be working with. Due to the classification of the things we were doing, our building was gated inside of the North Atlantic Treaty Organization (NATO) base.

My boss was a Navy lieutenant and my responsibility was to supervise two E-5s; one was Navy and the other Army. My responsibility was mainly to ensure that whatever we produced had the appropriate classification. Our lieutenant wanted us to be relaxed and productive, so he equipped the building with appropriate gym equipment and a kitchen. Most days, I went to work in authorized workout clothes. I worked out and then reviewed a few documents and checked my email, then had lunch and worked out again, and then did a final review of documents for the day. That was my routine for about four months, and it was the most laidback job I ever had as an E-6 in the Navy. The base was only an hour and fifteen minutes away from Amsterdam, and the main town was very nice and easy to get around. Once again, I met a few ladies and discovered that like most European countries, individuals learn more than one language. I met this one lady who didn't finish college, yet she spoke five languages fluently; she knew Dutch, English, Spanish, French, and German. That was so intriguing to me. How was that even possible and why? She said it was because they would get taught early on since they believed it was important to know many languages. Because the Netherlands is a small country, it needed to rely on partnerships with other nations. As good citizens, they all felt like it was their responsibility to learn other languages.

My time came to an end and I drove back to England, passing through the same countries as before but different cities. This was pivotal because it gave me a new love for adventure. I wanted to visit more cities in Europe and just explore, look for museums and landmarks, and all the best food each city had to offer. I got back to England and jumped into my work habits and personal habits. Again, I was seeing a bunch of ladies at once. One day, I was speaking with my mother and I told her a bit about my crazy times with a lady. She reminded me of a conversation we had when I was sixteen years old. Back then, I used to have girls call me and I would tell my brother to answer and say that I was not there or to stop calling. So my mother said to me, "Do you know that it's a woman who makes the choice? An average-looking woman gets hit on five to seven times daily. The man might not say let's go out or let's have sex right away, but if she is the one that turns around and says that to a complete stranger, he would react positively nine out of ten times. So the fact that a lady makes that choice, she chooses to give you her time and attention that means something." Like I said, this conversation was when I was sixteen so at that time, it didn't mean much since in my eyes I was the prince to those girls.

Now I was a twenty-seven-year-old man and she wanted to remind me of that conversation and how it was important to treat women right. I listened and understood, yet I was having too much fun. It was spring of 2009 and softball season was here, and I was part of the Navy team. We played a tournament between the different branches of the military and even different commands. During the tournament, I met two Air Force guys, one from Dominican Republic and another from Peru. We started hanging out and found Latin clubs all over England.

Also in the tournament was the boyfriend of the dental tech I first met when I checked in to the dental clinic in England—the one with the British accent. So I would see her because she came to watch him and us since we were on the same team. We did great as a team but, unfortunately, lost the championship game. I also started traveling that summer to places like Sevilla, Spain, Malta, plus more cities in England and lots of London visits.

In January 2009, all service members stationed in England got an email from the DoD asking for individuals who would like to be part of a movie. The email had details on how you had to follow military regulations like not wearing your current uniform and how you either participate on behalf of the Navy in my case or you could use your leave and get paid. I decided to enroll and take leave. The movie was Green Zone, starring Matt Damon. We had to travel to London and work for 8 hours, getting about 20 pounds sterling per hour and double for overtime. I did that for three days and then took a week's trip to Rabat, Morrocco for more filming. Morocco was full of vibrant colors, delicious food, and incredible places to see, we would work long hours so we only see the city at night, and we would eat at TGIF each evening where I would try a different dish each day. There we were shooting the entire time, and we met Matt Damon and the rest of the cast. I made some great memories and money, and learned that many Hollywood stars are short.

It was the summer of 2009, and I was at the gym. I noticed the dental tech and she was on her own. I saw her in the gym before, but her guy would be around, not working out, but just, like, checking on her like a bulldog. So I saw it as an opening. I approached her and said hi; she took her headphones off and I said, "Hey, how are you and where is your bulldog?" She had a huge smile and said, "I'm well and we're over, plus he left to the US." As she smiled, I said ok and smiled too. The next day, I emailed her at work and we started talking and seeing each other.

I was still seeing other people but I found myself seeing her more often. I canceled with others to be with her and even got jealous one time when I found a condom in her dresser. Yes, extremely hypocritical of me, but that's who I was back then. So without her telling me to do so, I started cutting ties with the other women and just spent my time with her. Getting to know her amazed me; I was impressed by her drive, her goals, and her desire to be the best version of herself. It's now Thanksgiving, 2009, and she invited me to have dinner with her family. She said it was nothing formal since other friends of hers would be at the dinner. I met her mom, and she was a funny and loving British lady. I also met her dad, a retired master sergeant of the Air Force.

We started talking, and within a few minutes he started schooling us. He first asked, "Are you guys investing in the Thrift Savings Plan (TSP)? If you're not, then you're missing out on the best retirement savings and investment plan out there since TSP offers the same type of savings and tax benefits that many private corporations offer their employees under so-called 401(k) plans, and the overhead, or paying ratio, is the best in the business." He said that since we got anywhere from a 1.5 to 2.4 percent raise each year, that we should increase our TSP contributions by at least 1 percent yearly. I was contributing maybe 2 percent at that point as well as having it in a plan with the lowest risk, the G Fund, which was the Government Securities Investment Fund. It was the most secure and least volatile option, but the one with the lowest return. I really loved how he talked about life, how he was open about his own personal issues and bouncing back, and how he was just down-to-earth.

During all that time, I still went to counseling for my PTSD. The counselor mentioned that I should visit the USS

Cole since I hadn't visited since I left in 2002. She said it would be healthy for me. I was debriefed on my yearly evaluation, and I was the #1 E-6 in my command. All my hard work had really paid off, and the chief advised that I should start looking for new orders and go back to a sea-going command. This way, I would get LPO and that would help me during the selection for E-7. Having all that information, I picked orders to the USS *Forrest Sherman* (DDG-98) out of Norfolk, VA. By now, I was only seeing the dental tech lady, Alicia. Only she had my attention until I received a message on Myspace from a Colombian lady that I really liked while on my deployment back in 2004. But back then she was seeing someone, just like I was. Well, now she was divorced and had a beautiful baby girl. I celebrated New Year's in London with my boys from the Air Force and one of the guys' wife. We had a really good time, but I also knew my time was short.

I was going to fly out around mid-February of 2010, and I was starting to get feelings for the lady I was seeing in England, but I also wanted to know what would happen with the Colombian lady. So I told Alicia that once I landed in the US, I was going to pursue the Colombian lady. Of course she didn't like that, but she just said, "Do you and thanks for being honest." In my eyes, it was just easier. She was going to school in San Antonio and I was going to be in Virginia, plus she was Air Force and I was Navy, which meant that it would be difficult to find a duty station we both could be in. So I was back on US soil in February 2010, and I was going to a school in Virginia before I met my ship, which was out on deployment.

I started dating the Colombian lady and things were amazing at first. She met my mom and my dad and part of my family. They all loved her because she was the first girlfriend that spoke Spanish since my high school days, so my mom truly enjoyed talking to her. Then it was her birthday and I took her out to dinner at a very nice restaurant. During the dinner, we started talking about our future and she said something that came as a surprise. She said, "I don't think I want to have any more children; my daughter messed up my body and I just don't want to go through that again." I was so disappointed and upset. So I said, "If you don't want to have children, then we're done. I can't be with someone that doesn't want to have children with me. Yes, you could change your mind later, but I don't want a maybe or I need to think. I want someone who is sure." So she got up and left, and our relationship ended. I was super sad because I liked her a lot but I wanted more children in my life.

Like a puppy with my tail between my legs, I started emailing Alicia, who was still in England but was going to be stationed in the US. We talked and I asked her for another chance. She said that she would come see me in Virginia, and if the vibes were good, then we could see where to go from there. The date is March of 2010, and I was doing great at my Navy school, plus spending time with my daughter and family before I had to meet my ship. Alicia showed up in April for about ten days. We spent the entire time together and she met my daughter. They hit it off right away, which was reassuring for me. After the ten days together, it was time for her to see family and report to her next duty station. As we said our goodbyes, I asked her if she would be my girl, and we made it official. It felt really good to have someone in my life that I could call mine and that would be there to love and support me even from a distance. May came, and I flew to hot Bahrain so I could meet the ship. It's 2010, and Bahrain was just as I remembered it when I left three years earlier—hot but lots of luxury. I was supposed to meet the ship out to sea in the Middle East, but the ship changed schedule and they pulled into Bahrain so I was able to meet them on the pier. There were four of us that were reporting to the ship, and we had all our seabags and luggage moving through the pier in that 100-degree weather. The ship was not completely moored, so everyone was topside and watching us come onboard. I felt like the new kid in school coming a few months after the school year started.

I changed into my uniform and headed to what would be my shop, radio, met a few of my coworkers, and then we headed to the flight deck because the Commanding Officer was going to do an all-hand call. During the all-hands, he discussed the success of the ship so far and he acknowledged the new individuals, like me. I got a lot of questions, like where did I come from, what was my rate or specialty, what was my hometown, etc. I met another Latino, he was a Logistics Specialist or LS, and he was so cool, not only super down-to-earth but also willing to help me understand a few things about the ship, the duty section, and just how things worked since I hadn't been part of a ship's crew for over seven or eight years. After a few days in Bahrain, it was time to head out to sea. I was not familiar with a lot of the systems onboard, so I had to be humble enough to tell the junior Sailors that I wasn't familiar with something or that I hadn't operated that equipment in years. That was not easy since as an E-6, there are high expectations for you by your upper chain of command and those Sailors working for you. I started to earn their trust by staying extra hours in the shop so I could get to know them, as well as the gear and responsibilities. There was so much to learn about maintenance cycles, requirements, and even qualifications.

I also had to relearn about damage control procedures, location of equipment, and important items. We hit a few ports, including beautiful Valencia, Spain. The city was so beautiful, with amazing beaches, food, and lots to do. It was there we proved that usually the best foods and drinks were found in a hole-in-the-wall restaurant—the places where the locals went to enjoy a meal. We found this mom-and-pop place that had the most amazing paella and sangria. Me and my boy just sat there for hours and had tapas, paella, and lots of sangria. Then we asked a cab driver about the best place to relax and have fun. He took us on a long drive to the outskirts of the city, and out of nowhere there it was. It looked like a playground for adults, with discos, houses for the ladies, and more. We only stayed in the clubs, but it was a great time since it was locals and only my group from the ship.

A couple of months later, we made it to back to Norfolk, Virginia. I was so happy to be back so I could see my daughter, my lady, my family, and friends. I saw my baby girl right away and a few days later, Alicia. She was still in another state going to school. She was doing everything she could to ensure that her next duty station would be in the same area as me. We knew it was going to be difficult because they usually only send you where you're needed, unless you're married. She also understood that if she did really well in school, she would have more of choice as a reward for her hard work. That made it easier for both of us since I was out to sea a lot and she could concentrate a lot more.

The year 2011 came, and we had more exercises and then prepared and executed inspection and survey (INSURV), which conducted acceptance trials of ships and service craft for the purpose of determining the quality of construction, compliance with specifications, and Navy requirements, to determine if equipment was operating satisfactorily. It was a lot of long hours and lots of stress since that inspection can get a Commanding Officer fired if the ship performs poorly or fails. After months of hard work and dedication by the entire crew, we passed with high marks. Those were the most challenging months as a leader until that point. I didn't have a Chief, so I was the acting Leading Chief Petty Officer, and I had to deal with the technical aspects of my shop but also all the personnel issues and responsibilities.

I was learning on the job, and because of that, I took a lot of hits and failures. I also was not the best leader as far as caring for the well-being of my Sailors. I was extremely demanding and never really satisfied because I expected everyone to give 100 percent every day, which is impossible. They had to do things how I wanted them to be done since if I do it this well or this fast, then they should be doing it as well. Then, I didn't understand that we all have a different level of 100 percent, which means that my 100 percent might be higher than others, but as a leader you have to understand what each of your team member's level is and just ensure you get whatever their 100 percent is for the day. That took years for me to understand, and I was not close to understanding that back in July of 2011. That month, my girlfriend was moving to Virginia. She was lucky and received orders to the same area as me, which was a blessing for my mental health and our relationship. I had the person that made me smile and was always supporting me in the same house, and I could expect to see her every day after a great day or a bad day.

In early August of 2011, I received news that I was selected for promotion to the rank of Chief Petty Officer. Getting that call was so unreal and amazing. I had so many emotions. Getting selected is one of the biggest milestones for an enlisted sailor since the Navy is the only branch of the military that makes that firm gap between the ranks of E-6 and below and E-7 and above. This meant that I would be going to Chief initiation, which consisted of seven weeks of training and guidance by the current Chiefs in my command. Six of us were selected, so we had to accomplish a bunch of daily, weekly, and capstone tasking while also dealing with our current responsibilities. Monday through Friday we had to workout starting at 04:30 a.m., which meant that the six of us had to be up by 03:30 a.m. and have everything ready no later than 04:15 a.m. We had to bring water and a healthy snack for the twenty-plus Chiefs who would be guiding us through the seven weeks. Our workout consisted of a lot of pushups and running two to three miles each day. Then we took the quickest shower ever and were ready to serve them breakfast. The chefs on the ship cooked the basic part of breakfast, like pancakes, breakfast potatoes, boiled eggs, etc.; but if one of the genuine Chiefs wanted eggs to order, we had to write down how they wanted it and with what ingredients and then one of the selects cooked it on the grill.

Thankfully for us, one of the selects was a cook so he knew his way around the galley, and even cooked little things that would make the genuine happy, like cinnamon rolls or waffles. From there, we cleaned up the Chiefs Mess and started our day, as far as operations, since we still had to run our divisions and take care of the mission and personnel. Then we would do it all over again for lunch and dinner. By the time we were done cleaning after dinner, it was 6:00 or 7:00 p.m. Then we would have to accomplish the daily tasking in relation to the season, and memorize the many things we were required to memorize. Most days, it would end at 10:00 p.m. or later and then we drove home, which for me was thirty to thirty-five minutes depending on traffic. A lot of days, I called my Fiancée just to tell her I wouldn't be coming home, since that allowed me to sleep an extra hour before starting over again at 03:30 a.m. the next day. Each day was more challenging, as you became more tired, would fail at accomplishing tasks, and we argued among ourselves because one or a few of us didn't accomplish a task on time or as required. Little did we know that it was all part of testing our resilience, our willingness to ask for help, our desire to do the right thing, and not completing a task, and most of all, how to work together toward a common goal.

One day, we left for the day but a hurricane warning was set and the entire ship was recalled, which meant that we all had to be back onboard the ship and be ready to go out to sea, since the ship would suffer more damage moored than it would ever suffer out to sea during a hurricane. At the start of the Chief season, we signed documentation that said that we would not drink alcohol during those seven weeks. We didn't understand why at first, but in time it was clear that with the lack of sleep, all the working out, and the little amount of food that we ate, drinking would be the worst thing we could do. Well, one of us selects had a few drinks in those two hours we were off the ship, so he was kicked out and lost the last four weeks of the season. It was only five of us going through it. Things just got harder after that because we had more tasking, but now we had one less person to help out. By the time we had to do what's called "final night," a series of events that lasted twenty-four hours ranging from running lots of miles to carrying heavy equipment with wet uniforms in the sand, I was so exhausted that my mind was not thinking right! But on September 16, 2011, I was accepted at 05:30 in the morning and my pinning ceremony was done onboard the USS *Forrest Sherman* (DDG-98) at 10:00 a.m. that same day.

It was surreal to be made and be accepted as a Chief Petty Officer on the same kind of ship where I became a true sailor, a guided missile destroyer (DDG). My daughter and Alicia were there and I saw how proud they were to see me get my anchors. It's also cool to note that as I made my first salute as a Chief, my fiancée, who would soon be commissioned as an Air Force Officer, saluted me back. After that, the ship finally left the yards and was ready to go back out to sea. This meant that I was going to be away from home and I had to plan this accordingly.

CHAPTER XI

I got married in December of 2011. It was a very small ceremony but it was exactly what we both wanted, because we believed in spending our money on us and not on a huge wedding for others to enjoy. Before we got married, I had to come clean about an ugly secret, something I was ashamed to talk about and that nobody would have guessed due to my appearance. I was in debt badly, not counting my car debt, which was big since I had a brand-new fully loaded ES350 Lexus, and over 17k in credit card and personal loan debt. After I proposed and she said yes, Alicia waited a few days and asked me about my finances and my credit score. I was so upset that she asked but only because I knew she wouldn't like it. I requested and printed my three reports and was able to see all the accounts, debt, and credit score, which was horrible at 580. What was really troublesome was that my clearance for my job depended on having a good financial situation, and I was far from it. Thankfully, she was patient with me and we came up with a plan. I was going on deployment soon, so she sold her vehicles and kept the profits. Then she said she would drive my car while I was underway but send me the vehicle payment. I would use that money plus another $800 from my salary to pay the debt, and I had to close a few accounts and leave all but one credit card with her.

Using those measures, we determined that it would take me thirteen months to clear the debt. That became my number one goal while on deployment, put money into the debt each month. My debt went down and my credit score went up, so I paid it all off in eight months. That was a very valuable learning experience, learning about trusting others and working toward goals together. Those eight months were spent on deployment, and before I left on deployment, in July of 2012, my wife and I negotiated orders to commands in Florida. Each base was 80 miles apart, so we moved to a town that was located almost smack in the middle. Before I headed out to sea, we drove down from Virginia to Florida and got her settled since she was going to be alone for the next six months. I took a flight back to Virginia and left on deployment. I was only supposed to stay until November of 2012, but as November got closer, I noticed that my relief was not identified yet. This was extremely frustrating for me because I had made the proper calls, messages, and the official channels of communication were all utilized to ensure everyone was aware that I didn't have a replacement.

It was extremely difficult to deal with the feeling of helplessness since I knew my chain of command was not going to allow me to depart the ship without a replacement. It was frustrating to know that the Navy had advanced over 150 Information Systems Technicians to Chief, and one of them should have been my replacement. I know for a fact that from October of 2012, when I was told I was not getting a relief anytime soon, until the time I did in February of 2013, I was the worst leader I could have ever been. No matter what my Sailors did, it made me angry or triggered me and I talked to them in a way that was not caring or respectful. Every day, I woke up angrier than the last. I hated any drill or training evolution because I saw it as worthless. I just wanted to go home, but due to our operational requirement of staying off the coast of Syria just in case things escalated and also to shoot missiles, I knew it was not happening. I was miserable for those months, and I know my Sailors and anybody that had to interact with me felt my cruel words and actions. When my relief finally came, I had two weeks to do the best turnover of responsibilities as possible, but she was interested in visiting the port in Italy. That's when it hit me that I was leaving my Sailors in the hands of someone who wouldn't care as much as I did or even hold them to high standards like I did, and that made me feel sad. But it was also time to move on, and as I said earlier, by that point I was too cruel and angry to them so it was for the best.

In mid-March of 2013, I was reunited with my beautiful wife, Alicia, in sunny Florida and it felt amazing. Now that she was used to her job and I was working on shore duty, aka no more sea time or deployment for the next three years, we talked about starting our family and having a baby. I wanted a boy so bad, mostly because I already had my beautiful princess and now I wanted a prince. I think I it was too much pressure on my wife, so she decided that we wouldn't find out the sex until the baby was born. I thought that was going to be torture, but to my surprise after the first couple of months of us finding out that she was pregnant, it became super easy to not think about it. It was even fun buying a lot of unisex things for the house and the baby. We talked about names, and it had to be two names, two middle names, etc. It was also fun answering questions from those that couldn't understand how we could be so calm and cool about not finding out the sex of the baby.

In February of 2014, our baby was born. I was in the room this time, and I was able to see the doctor pull the baby out and see what sex it was. To my surprise, it was a boy! I was overcome with emotion and I started crying; I was so happy and just in love! I called my mother right away and I cried even more. I cried so much while talking to my mother that she asked me if the baby was ok. I told her yes and that I was just emotional because I wanted a boy so bad. My baby boy was full of energy, very funny, and loving. I loved getting him ready in the morning or feeding him and bathing him after work. I gave him kisses on the cheeks or tummy or chunky legs any chance I got; it made me so happy to see him smile and just be full of joy.

We were a happy family and things were going amazing at work and with us, but I was not feeling satisfied intimately. I felt like I always had to be the one to start things and try to be romantic or just sensual. In my head, I was doing everything a man is supposed to do. I gave her compliments about a change on her hairstyle or color, new nails, new perfume, or anything different because I paid attention to details. I listened and got her a gift on a weekday just because I heard her say she liked something. I brought or sent flowers or edible arrangements just because it was Tuesday. We paid for maids and a gardener so we didn't have to worry about that. I helped with cooking and laundry. I did dishes and folded clothes, and I loved doing anything for my baby boy, yet I felt like I was not a priority.

I might have communicated my concerns or disappointment once or twice, but I didn't make it a "let's sit down and figure this out" kind of priority. So I started to cheat, with the excuse that she was not making me happy. I started to seek more and more satisfaction from others. I just kept telling myself, "It's her fault I am here now. If she listened and pleased me, this wouldn't be happening."

It's taken me a while to try to come up with excuses as to why I was unfaithful. All those things I mentioned before were true. I did do all those things for her, and I tried to make our lives better and make her feel loved every opportunity I had. The therapist I was seeing years later made me reflect and think about the things I was not doing. I didn't give her quality time because I would be sitting next to her but on my phone checking social media or watching sports. I didn't try to listen to what she might have been missing. Above all, if I was unhappy then I should have asked for a divorce, instead of cheating and making her suffer.

I look back and ask myself, "Why didn't I say what was bothering me? How was she supposed to know how I felt?" I truly don't have the answer, even today. I just think I wanted to be with other women, so no matter what she did, I was going to find a reason to cheat. I say that because I was cheating recklessly. I was doing things at work and with women who were in marriages and relationships. I don't say that to sound like I was doing something big or cool; I say it to note how bad I was living. I was just doing things with no regard to my family, to my profession, and just being selfish because I was satisfying my needs at all costs. My wife found out in March of 2015 and we were divorced by July of 2015. Thankfully, she had so much grace that she was not trying to be vindictive by asking for all this money or stuff. She asked for what my son needed, and I was happy to sign whatever because I knew it was for him. So I didn't ask for anything in the house besides a couple of things, and I didn't mind the amount for child support and childcare, even if she made about 30 percent more than me. We both agreed not to tell the military about us filing for divorce so we could negotiate for orders in the same location. As far as they were concerned, we were still married and needed to be in the same location. Thankfully, it worked out and we both were going to work in Virginia next.

I reported to Virginia in August of 2015, now as a Senior Chief Petty Officer. I would be leading and influencing more Sailors due to my position in the command as the Senior Enlisted Leader and Communication Officer. One of the pleasant surprises of the new job was that I would be the Immediate Superior in Command (ISIC) for the USS *Cole*. My job as an ISIC was for assigned ships to prepare them for sustained combat operations at sea. I prepared ships for assignment to operational commanders as directed by the commander. It was very therapeutic and rewarding to come back onboard the *Cole* to do inspections or just simply check on Sailors. The ship had different ways to honor those that died during the bombing, like seventeen stars on the floor that takes you from the food serving area to the sitting area of the cafeteria. There were plaques of the individuals at their workplace onboard the ship back when the bombing occurred, and even more impressive, there was a huge sense of pride and responsibility from the crew. `

The USS *Cole* is part of Naval history, and those that get stationed on the ship inherit the honor of setting the standard for other ships to emulate. I was extremely focused on the new job, but I still wanted to get my ex-wife back. I went to marriage counseling to see if they could help me get her back. She agreed to go on a couple of dates with me because she wanted to start over but also date others, leaving her options open. As I spoke with the counselor at each session, I discovered a few things. I learned about the love languages. Here I was, a 35-year-old man, and it was the first time I heard about that concept and learned which ones were my love languages and even identified which ones were hers. I also learned that for us to have a chance again, I would have to be completely honest about all the dirty that I did. As much as I wanted her back, I understood that it would be too much for her to forgive. If she would have done what I did, I would have never forgave her or trusted her, so why it would be any different for her? The last thing I realized was that we would still have different opinions, and they were important to her and to me but just not aligned. So why try to settle just for the sake of keeping our family together?

We went on dates, we tried in a few aspects but around January of 2016, we had the final conversation and I realized that she would never forgive me. Even if she only knew the minimum, she would never trust me. I didn't tell her everything that did happen, even if my counselor said that I should have. Why? No benefit would have come from it, because I knew she would never forgive me, no matter if it was one or ten women I cheated with. I give her a bunch of credit because she was able to admit that to herself and to me. She explained to me that she loved seeing me with my son and how happy he would be and how she would want to have the family completed, but she just couldn't trust me. She said she would need all my passwords and would be checking my phone, email, and social media without knowing for how long and she didn't want to live that way or even put me through that. I truly respected her views because I could tell it was not words out of anger or vindictiveness; it was someone who was calm and completely understood what was important to her. It took a few more months for me to get it and it hurt to see her dating someone, specifically as he became the main person and then the boyfriend and more. With time, I appreciated the fact that she was happy and he was a great guy and someone that I could trust to be around my son. My ex-wife would never put her happiness above our son; she would only date someone that was worth it as a man and as a future stepfather.

My focus was on working and going to school. I had put off going to college for too long. I always found a way or reason to get discouraged or just stopped after finishing a class. So while I was stationed in Florida, my ex-wife used to say, "How can you demand from your children and Sailors to put education as a priority if you haven't?" So I was at the college office the next day. At first, I asked for a college plan for a Bachelor's Degree and once I saw the amount of credits I had to get, I was completely discouraged, like before. Thankfully, the lady who helped me saw my dissolution and suggested I go for an Associate's Degree and recommended a school that took as many of my Navy classes as possible. After that review, I only needed seven classes to get my associates, and all those credits would roll over to the next university for my bachelors.

School was really a challenge after all those years not attending school, having a baby, and the responsibilities of my job. Thankfully, I really enjoyed the subjects, since they were all in the same field as my work in the Navy. I completed my associates in December of 2014. Now that I was settled in my next command, I decided to enroll for my bachelors. It was October of 2015, and I balanced my work schedule, school, and seeing my two kids. I had a lot of help from each of their mothers, both with time and money. They understood that I was going out to sea a lot more. So if it was my turn to have my kids this weekend but I was going to be out to sea, then when I returned, I would have them for two weekends in a row or whatever worked for all of us. For the money part, I paid child support to each and childcare. And they didn't ask for more at every chance, which allowed me to take my children on trips and adventures. So for those things and more, I'm extremely grateful to never having baby momma drama. The reason why I didn't and will never call them baby momma is because for me, they're more. Both are amazing women, mothers, and service members, who both have master's degrees and are professionals, and I will respect them as such always.

January of 2016 was truly a new beginning for me. I was finally ok with being divorced and both of us moving on with our lives. My focus was spending as much time as I could with my daughter, who was fourteen now, and my son, who was two. I had them both every other weekend, and we did lots of fun things, like going to museums, movies, parks, driving to Jersey to see grandma, aka Abuela, and much more. I asked to have them even on weekends that I was not supposed to have them, just because I knew soon I would be out to sea on a deployment. At the end of 2016, I was preparing for a seven-to-eight-month deployment, starting in January of 2017. Unfortunately, my ex-wife was going to deploy as well, so we had to figure out where our three-year-old son was going to stay. Thankfully, her parents took on the massive responsibility of caring for a baby while they both worked. I said it before but I will say it again, the love and appreciation I have for my son's grandparents can only be compared to the love and appreciation I have for my mother. Not only did they take care of my baby boy, but he flourished with them and we were informed and included in all his little milestones.

January 2017 came and it was time to deploy. I knew that I was going to be moving a lot from the carrier to my destroyers for a couple of reasons—I wanted to check on the crew of each ship and I also wanted to check for whatever inspections I was required to do as the ISIC. Our first port visit was Souda Bay, in Greece. I found another Chief that had the same interests as me, which was to get a really nice hotel room and chill in our rooms, with room service and the ability to contact our families.

I didn't have to stand duty, so I called to check in since I was the Senior Enlisted Leader, but for the most part I was away. While in Souda, I scheduled a massage in my room for two hours and it was amazing. I used the rooftop pool and just reenergized. After four days, it was back out to sea and I developed a routine. I worked out after all the morning meetings, which lasted until about 9:45 to 10:00, then I worked out for an hour and fifteen to twenty minutes. During that workout, I ran five miles, at least, plus weights. Then I showered and ate lunch. I worked from 1:00 p.m. to around 3:30 p.m. and hit the gym again for another hour, plus ran another five miles and lifted more weights. Then I ate dinner before working from 6:30 p.m. to around 9:30 p.m. I did that every day, with the exception of Sunday.

One beautiful thing about deployments was that you could get into a routine easily. Since each day was Monday for us, we knew the schedule for the week, with minor changes here and there. So it was easy to see which meetings I needed to be at or what brief I had to produce reading material for or just read ahead. Then every two to three weeks, I scheduled a flyover to one of my destroyers that was close by. I took one of the anti-sub helicopters and asked them to patrol the area where they would fly me to the other ship. On one occasion, we had a distress call, and what supposed to be a thirty-minute trip from the destroyer back to the carrier turned into a five-hour operation. All I could do was watch because I was not qualified to use any of the equipment onboard, since it was not part of my rate job description. After about a month plus out to sea, we made it to our next port visit, the Kingdom of Bahrain. It was good to be back and see all the changes, plus having the liberty to stay in nice hotels and just relax again. Another four days spent relaxing, eating well, and pampering myself with manicures, pedicures, massages, a haircut, and buying tailor-made suits. Then it was time to head out again. We stayed in the region for a few months, and I visited other destroyers as well as went back to Bahrain with one of the ships that needed me to stay onboard a bit longer for inspection purposes. I made it back to the carrier, and within a couple of weeks, we were going to moored in Dubai, UAE. I had visited Dubai before on other deployments, so it was not a surprise. Again, since I was a higher-ranking sailor, this time I had more privilege and money to get the high-end hotels.

I was extremely grateful for my buddy since I could count on him to go out with me. In the Navy we are big on utilizing the buddy system while overseas. There were groups of at least two people but no more than five, with one person within the group who would be the nondrinker for at least one period of 24 hours, or the entire time the group was out. I spoke with my kids each day, even if that meant me staying up late or waking up super early to make sure it was during the time they were up. After another month in that Area of Responsibility, or AOR, we made our way back to the Mediterranean, which meant hitting ports in Europe, and to me they were the best. Before hitting any port, I was assigned to test some capabilities on a Danish ship. We wanted to know: if something happened to one of our destroyers, could a team of US Sailors embark the Danish ship and perform the same functions expected of a destroyer within a strike group? The name of the ship was HMDS *Peter Willemoes*, who was a highly advanced Danish Frigate capable of sustained war fighting against air, surface, and subsurface threats all while having five star cuisine, Wi-Fi, and accommodations. The team was there for eight days and the things we experienced compared to US ships were incredible. The Danish Navy is not as large as the US's, so they're able to invest more money into technology and equipment since they have about ten ships total. They also are able to train their personnel better because they go to technical school and college as well as work on the same kind of ship year after year, so they truly become subject-matter experts.

As I walked around the ship, I saw that the quality of life for these Sailors included such luxuries as four-man staterooms with an attached bathroom, a game/arcade area, and a pub onboard for port calls to reduce in-town incidences. The cooks were trained in countries like Spain and France, and they had a butcher onboard and a pastry chef.

The crew was integrated with electronic monitored engineering systems and triple redundancies, which allowed for a smaller crew and much higher efficiency. After about four days out to sea, the *Willemoes* pulled in to Limassol, Cyprus, and it was gorgeous. I stayed in an amazing hotel and since I was one of the few US Sailors in town, I was on my own. So I just relaxed and enjoyed the time by the beach or at the pool, ate at the fanciest restaurants I could find, and got a massage almost daily. We left Limassol, and our team was flown to the carrier so we could continue our support for that area. Then, about three weeks later, we were pulling into Haifa, Israel. While in Israel, we took tours to the Dead Sea, Jerusalem, and Bethlehem. Visiting those places with so much history and religious significance was something out of dreams, not because I'm religious or anything, but just seeing people's reactions was moving. Walking the streets of Israel made you feel like you were witnessing history; the city was very modern, but they kept anything that was significant intact. Every day, I found myself walking or seeing something from thousands of years ago. Then you turn, and you're in a super modern coffee shop, with military personnel walking around with M16 rifles like they were carrying a cell phone; very surreal. After a few days enjoying the cities and culture, it was time to go into the next part of the deployment, which involved an exercise with a carrier from Great Britain and a French Destroyer.

A couple of us were flown out from the carrier to Naples, Italy, so we could take a flight into London, England, and participate in a conference that lasted a couple of days. During that time in England, I took two other colleagues to a futbol, or soccer, match. We got tickets to see Arsenal at their home stadium and it was an awesome atmosphere; they loved it. We flew back to the carrier and did the exercise for a few weeks before we moored in Portsmouth, England. We had another great time, and I talked to my children, which made my life as complete as it could be while on a deployment. I was also extremely happy that my son's mother was already back from her deployment so that made me feel better because my boy had his mom back. I returned home to Virginia in August of 2017, and my daughter was waiting for me at the pier. We missed each other and once I found her, we hugged probably the longest we ever had, and I loved every second of it.

To celebrate, I had planned a trip to London and Paris with my daughter, now fifteen. It was another trip in our series of exploring the world together. In 2015, I had planned a trip to Barcelona with my wife at the time, but a month prior she found out that I had cheated on her and she was not trying to go anywhere with me. To her credit, she suggested that I take my daughter instead. She said that I should be doing trips with her, just the two of us, so we could connect deeper and build memories. So I took my princess, and we had a blast going to FC Barcelona VIP style, used the hop-on/hop-off bus for two days, and just enjoyed all the sights and food. We made so many amazing memories that I made it a point to make it a yearly thing. I asked her for a list of places she would like to go around the world, and she didn't disappoint. The next city we selected was Rio de Janeiro. She wanted to go there because of the movie *Rio*, and I wanted to return since I visited before, but this time I wanted to do more exploring.

In March of 2016, we flew to Rio and stayed at the Hilton that was used for the 2014 World Cup and would be used for the Summer Olympics. We had so much fun exploring the city, eating at Michelin restaurants and mom-and-pop restaurants, and enjoying the sights. We made memories from the airport to the Christ the Redeemer. As I said before, in 2017 after deployment, we did Paris and London, more sightseeing, and lots of food. While on that vacation, I was informed that I was going to get stationed/moved to Sicily, Italy. I was super disappointed and upset because I was building a new house. I had asked to stay in the Virginia area, and I knew how difficult it would be to see my children from that distance. We still made the best of it, and as soon as we got back to the US, I started figuring out when I had to report and planned our next trip before I was going to live in Sicily. We agreed on Costa Rica, mostly because we wanted to see all the greenery, volcanoes, and beautiful beaches. October of 2018 was here, and we embarked on our journey to Costa Rica and it was super fun. I made sure to get a travel agent to book the right hotels and book excursions, like zip lining, ATVs, a chocolate factory tour, and transportation between venues and hotels. We stayed in two different locations within Costa Rica, one by the volcanoes and one by the jungle. The other hotel was by the beach and both had unique highlights. We returned from Costa Rica, and soon enough I was packing my belongings and shipping my car to Sicily to start that new chapter.

CHAPTER XII

Ilanded in Sicily upset because I didn't want to be there. My desire was to stay in Virginia so I could be close to my son and daughter. So I requested to go back-to-back sea duty, but I was told that I was needed at the command in Sicily due to the mission, which was very satellite communication heavy and that was my bread and butter, my Navy Enlisted Classification (NEC) and the fact that the billet had been gapped for over eighteen months. I understood the mission and why I was selected for those orders even if I did not request to come to Sicily. I settled in a beautiful apartment, with a pool, volleyball court with beach sand, and an amazing gym. My landlord was an awesome older Sicilian man; he got me a pizza and a soda on the day I paid the rent and invited me to have dinner with his family monthly. Those dinners were a feast but also super long between the appetizers, pasta, meat, fish, veggies, and dessert with wine. It would take three hours or more. I was still very grateful that I was invited and that I was able to experience that.

Thankfully, my desire to see Europe clicked in, and I made it a mission to travel every three or four-day weekend, which happened at least once a month. I planned to visit cities that I hadn't visited or visit two that were my favorites ever, Barcelona and Oslo. Then I found a soccer match and visited that city. While there, I visited museums, ate local foods, and saw any interesting places in the city. Then I watched the soccer match and explored some more. By January of 2019, I had already visited Madrid, Lisbon, Oslo, and Barcelona. Next, I was going to Cambridge so I could spend time with my son for his birthday in February. I also worked on a few qualifications that I needed to make myself more competitive for the next pay grade. Although I was doing so well and seeing so many wonderful places, I was still feeling a bit down. So I made an appointment with a psychiatrist, and we started talking about why I was feeling down as well as why I was such a womanizer. I was back to seeing three or four women at once. We talked about understanding that I would have down days if I only found happiness when I traveled or did something adventurous that day. I understood that was not possible to sustain. So on days that were just a regular day, what things was I doing to love myself and take care of myself? He provided tools, reading materials, and techniques to apply in those situations. He suggested I take on work challenges that would benefit morale since he knew how important that was to me. He also suggested having measurable goals at the gym instead of just going just to say I was there. Another suggestion was to write about my children, not to show them later necessarily, but for me to really express my love by describing them. I started applying those suggestions and I felt so much better and learned about myself.

The aspect we discussed was my constant desire to be liked by women; my desire to sleep with as many women as I could, and, even worse, not caring about their feelings as long as I was getting what I wanted. Like most psychiatrists, he asked questions about my childhood and that explained some of it, like my desire to be liked and praised. Then he asked if I'd ever been raped, sexually assaulted, or sexually harassed. I had never shared that I was sexually assaulted back in 2001 by a male Chief, so I was nervous about admitting that to him, even though I knew it was the only way he could help me. I didn't say anything that time and lied. But a few sessions later, I felt the need to say everything so he could truly help me become a better person since I finally looked for healing. I explained to him that the Chief told me to get undressed, and then he did what he wanted and I just froze. I told the psychiatrist that I was so scared to move and then later report him because he said, "Nobody is going to believe a Seaman, and I'm a Chief." But worse I was scared that people would call me gay since I didn't fight him. When this happened, in 2001, I was extremely homophobic due to the belief that it was wrong due to my upbringing in the Catholic faith and Church as well as how all I heard growing up was how disgusting that was. So I didn't want anybody to know because I had to be gay to let a man do that to me. The psychiatrist explained how I was looking for validation all these years since I needed to conquer as many women as possible to prove to myself that I was a man. He then encouraged me to report it, and I said, "Why? He is long retired." And he said, "Because it's important that you let go, that you don't feel guilty for something HE did." I said ok because I felt guilty that he probably did it to others after me, and I could have reported him back then and stopped him from hurting others.

This process was not easy; it took a lot of sessions and conversations on how to approach each scenario. One of the biggest issues my counselors identified was how much I lied just to get a woman in bed, and how I lied about my availability because the more women I was with, the more I felt like a man. Deep down I wanted to make sure I was not gay by having as many women as possible, and the fact that they did not know anything about the sexual assault did not matter to me. I never gave these ladies the opportunity to make a choice, the choice of saying no or yes to sleeping with someone that was sleeping with other women. This was a bad habit that was not easy to just kick to the side. Unfortunately, for every two ladies I asked to see me, only one would get all the details on how I was living my life; the other one I just lied to. As I write this, I recognize how awful I was and how dangerous I was living since for the most part, I was not using protection. Time and time again, I felt bad and worried. So I got tested and, thankfully, it always came back clean. Although, back in 2002, I had a scare with chlamydia. I was lucky enough that I was able to get tested and treated quickly, and never had it again.

In 2019, I was still traveling all over Europe. I saw VIP concerts in Zurich, Switzerland, ate a seven-course chef's table meal at a restaurant with three Michelin stars, and celebrated New Year's at the rooftop of a famous hotel in Stockholm, Sweden. I was still making strides in the command, changing the culture of my department by demanding more, holding all of us accountable, and thinking that taking care of my Sailors meant more than just taking care of them on Navy-related issues. The satisfaction I got from seeing them reach levels that they didn't think were possible was the fuel that allowed me to work long hours or go to them on the weekends to talk and laugh with my watch standers and even bring something to eat. Then, in early 2020, I met someone that would forever change my perspective about relationships. I learned to trust your partner and love someone for who they are.

It was a cold morning in January of 2020, and I was heading to the gym as I usually did. I saw from the corner of my eye the amazing legs of a beautiful lady that was doing circuit training with a kettlebell. I didn't like to interrupt or even talk to ladies while they worked out, so I just waited for after the workout, but I missed her and she was gone. A few days later, we were both heading into the gym from the parking lot, so I finally had the time and courage to say something. I asked what brought her to Sicily, and she said she was stationed here as well. Then we spoke about our workout goals and routine for the day. After our workout, I saw her in the parking lot already changed and ready to head to work.

So I asked her, "Can I have your number?" Then I gave her a big smile.

"Yes, my number is . . ." she said.

For a few weeks, our conversations were short and just over text, but one evening it was her birthday and she asked:

"Have you danced on a rooftop under the moon before?"

"No, but I would love to with you," I said.

She sent me her address and I was there about an hour later. We headed to the rooftop and the moon was super bright and we had mystic clouds around us, and we danced salsa, merengue, and bachata for a while. Then we went down to her apartment and kissed very passionately, and, well, you know what happened after. After only two hours of sleep or less, it was time for me to go to work, and I left. We talked throughout the day about the experience and how unique everything was. I already had scheduled dinner with another woman, so I asked if I could see her a few days later, and, thankfully, she said yes. The next time we saw each other, we didn't talk much to start. After all the excitement, we both finally started talking about the other variables that would shape whatever it was we were trying to do. She talked about how private she was, so she didn't want anything to be said or shown at the base or at her job. That was cool with me since I liked to keep my personal life as private as possible.

Next, she told me that she was in a serious relationship. She said he was in the US but knew what she was doing with me and others. That shocked me. First, because the way she acted with me intimately didn't give me any hint that she was with anybody, let alone someone super serious as she said they were. Second, she said me and others, which meant that she was sleeping with other guys now or before me. At that moment, I asked the question, "Are you sleeping with other guys right now?" And she said yes. She started talking about the different individuals, where they were located, and if it was a one-time thing or something that's regular enough to compete with our time. The most disturbing part was how bad I felt, yet I was doing the exact same thing. I even judged her. I asked, "So you're sleeping with all these guys without them knowing about it beforehand and also unprotected, like us?" She just looked at me and said, "Well, you didn't ask about both, so I didn't say anything but now that you're asking, I'm telling you all the details so you know what I'm about."

I still couldn't believe it, even if she was just the female version of me. So we discussed more and came to the agreement that we would continue to do what we were doing between each other and with others. If something changed, then we would communicate that change—like when she traveled to another country and stayed at a stranger's house. She met him on a website about couch surfing, and they ended up having sex. Once again, I was upset and I judged. I demanded answers like I was her boyfriend, when in reality I was number two at best. Then late March 2020 happened; COVID happened. This forced us to only see each other because we couldn't travel to other towns, cities or countries. In Sicily, a government order came out that stated all citizens could only transit from home to work and back. You could go to supermarkets, pharmacies, hospitals, and gas stations only if they were en route between work and home. Military personnel had to carry a document written in English and Italian that explained the individual's duty and work/home addresses. Luckily for me, her address was on the main highway I used to get home.

Since we only saw each other outside of work, we started doing more stuff together, things that were not part of what she was allowed to do in her open relationship. I was staying in her house more often than not. I had my own towel, toothbrush, soap, and even groceries. We cooked for each other and watched movies and shows, and that kind of became our thing. Of course, with all that time together, we shared things about our lives. Since I was still very insecure about myself and what I meant to her, I asked about her sexual escapades and then judged her. She told me about her threesomes, unplanned or planned orgies, random meet-ups, or sleeping with different people. Her honesty and vulnerability should have been applauded, understood, and taken as a sign of her trust and commitment to me.

There were a lot of arguments and tears from both sides because we were both trying to be as honest and raw as possible; sometimes that hurt, especially for me, but it's what I needed. I needed to be ok with emotions; the truth is always better, no matter how it might make you or others feel. In the mix of all of those personal emotions, I was also working on my professional goals. One of the biggest qualifications that I was missing to get my specialty in the Navy was the Joint Fleet Telecommunications Operations Center Watch Officer (JFTOCWO). The JFTOCWO was a 24/7 one-stop shop for C5I (command, control, communications, computers, collaboration, and intelligence) needs. JFTOC interacted with the fleet and joint customers via message traffic, chat, phone, or Video Tele-Conference (VTC). JFTOC was the "Battle Watch Captain" for troubleshooting fleet communications outages of a specific Area of Responsibility.

I was also working on my master's degree in Information Technology Management. Around July of 2020, I applied for an Applied Cyber Operations (MACO) program, which was a program that allowed E-6 and above Sailors the opportunity to enroll in the Naval Postgraduate School (NPS), a 15-month master's program that was one of many efforts to increase cyber capabilities for the Navy while building a professional cyber workforce. The Applied Cyber Operations curriculum was intended to provide a deep understanding of the implementation of national and military application of integrated lines of operations, including the DoD Information Network Operations (DoDINOps), Defensive Cyberspace Operations (DCO), Offensive Cyberspace Operations (OCO), cyber security fundamentals, and the required technical operations underpinning these. I didn't think I was going to be selected, since I was already at almost twenty years in the Navy. Surprisingly, I was selected, and I had to report by March of 2021 to embark on my next adventure as a full-time student while still getting paid by the Navy at my current pay grade.

My relationship with the lady in Sicily continued to get stronger, but two things remained: we both had to get back to the US and go on separate paths, and she was still very much involved and in love with her boyfriend, who was waiting in America. We still found time to escape the island and visited places like Turin, Matera, and Bari in Italy. Each trip allowed us to enjoy the simple things and continue to grow together and individually.

COVID took a lot away from all of us, but one of the biggest things it took away was my ability to fly to the US and see my daughter graduate from high school in June of 2020. I had missed so many things through the years, and I had promised her that I would be there no matter what. Unfortunately, I didn't put a pandemic into consideration. I tried to request permission to fly back since we were in heavy quarantine again, but due to the fourteen days of isolation once I landed in America, the time there, and then fourteen days once I landed in Sicily, my command would not grant the permission required. It's one of the biggest regrets of my life; I needed to be there! My princess deserved that much and I failed. I tried to explain it to her and she said that she understood, but I knew it hurt her. I knew she was happy to be done with high school, so it was a milestone and a relief that I had wished to share with her.

Around October of 2020, the limitations due to COVID started to disappear and a normal routine started to happen. Yes, we still needed to have our face mask, but we were able to do more, which included traveling. Now it's January of 2021, and we finally got the first vaccines in Sicily and I was one of the first ones who volunteered to take it. I was a bit nervous but ready to do my part by taking the step of protecting myself with the vaccine. Plus, I was going back to the US the next month, so it was important to me that I was protected and not spreading the virus at any cost. In February of 2021, I landed in Virginia after transferring from Sicily en route to Monterey, California, for fifteen months of school. I wanted to see my family after sixteen months of not seeing my children or my mother, so I spent time in New Jersey, Connecticut, and Virginia, and drove down to Florida to see my mother and best friend. Then I continued my drive, stopping in cities just to sleep so I could get as many leave and travel days with my son, who was living in Vegas and was now seven years old. I spent eight days with him before I continued my drive to Monterey. We did so much, from going into the pool at the hotel daily to museums, aquarium, parks, and ate lots of yummy food. I arrived in Monterey, and I was able to get my apartment keys right away since I had done all the research and paperwork online.

It was a small one-bedroom apartment, but it was in a great city called Pacific Grove, which was only six miles away from the school campus. The complex had a beautiful pool and a nicely equipped gym. I was about a week early to my report day of March 25, 2021, but that time was used wisely since I received my home goods shipment, had internet connected, and all the other services required as well as finding out where all the main stores were located. I quickly realized that if I wanted to see any sporting events, concerts, or just have more diversity in the restaurant choices, I would have to drive an hour to hour and half to San Jose, San Francisco or Oakland.

My first semester was all virtual, with some classes recorded from the semester before, and we had to watch it at our convenience even if we had class time scheduled during the week. This was an unpleasant situation since it just gave me more reason to stay lazy. There was no real human interaction, since we only spoke in some classes that were done live, and it was hard to get answers about things I didn't understand at the moment. You had to email the professor and hope he/she replied before the assignment was due. Before the start of my second semester, I met Emily, who lived in another state; we met in a group on Facebook, and we started meeting in different places in the US. We saw some beautiful cities and stayed at amazing hotels. She also helped me with my schoolwork, mostly proofreading my papers and assignments, since I still had issues with words and punctuation. Thankfully, the second semester was in person, because the classes had gotten harder, and I really needed to move around a lot more because I put on weight and felt lazy as well as a bit depressed.

A byproduct of having to be on campus was having to dress a certain way due to a dress code, so I purchased more polo shirts, dress pants, and comfortable dress shoes. I always enjoyed dressing well, but this gave me an extra opportunity to get a classier and more sophisticated look. Unfortunately, while in school, I learned that my son's mother was moving to England for her next duty station. One of the reasons I applied to the MACO program was because I would be closer to him since he was in Vegas. So I made it a priority to see him a few times before they left, and we had some amazing time together and made beautiful memories. It's now October of 2021, and the third semester was underway, which meant harder classes and the beginning of my research and writing my thesis. On the personal side, the lady I was seeing in Sicily was now in the US, so I saw her a couple of times and it was clear that although a lot of old connection sexually was there, she had moved on emotionally. So we just saw each other as friends that enjoyed intimacy with each other.

My thesis was going to focus on a system that would help the Navy with automation to combat cyber threats. I had to have my thesis ready for review by February 1 since I was graduating at the end of March. So by January of 2022, I was already done with all the research, testing of the virtual environment, and writing. Here is the executive summary with some minor changes:

The CWS (Cyber Warfighting System) project evaluates the tools and procedures to detect and declare an active cyber threat and establish the proper readiness postures to respond. The project has evolved into a series of phases. Phase I evaluated the performance of an automated Endpoint Detection and Response (EDR) tool against an adversary emulation plan based on an Advanced, Persistent Threat (APT) using the MITRE ATT&CK framework. Phase II evaluated the performance of SOAR tools compared to a standalone SIEM device. The results confirmed the benefit of using automated custom playbooks, which are predefined logical procedures, to enhance intelligence and block threats in a shipboard environment isolated from shore support. Phase III will assess the impact of automation, human-in-the-loop, and playbooks, in defensive cyber operations (DCO) from ashore to afloat in a disconnected and intermittent bandwidth environment.

Phase III, Stage 1 will set up the testing environment. Testing during Phase III, Stage 2 will assess the effectiveness of security technologies such as SOAR, SIEM, and EDR to counter a series of cyber threat actions within a simulated shipboard environment. My thesis focuses on Phase III, Stage 1, and defines a method for Phase III, Stage 2 of the CWS project. In Phase III, Stage 1, the capstone produced a series of workflows that will enable testing of the cyber incident response (IR) capabilities of select tools and playbooks within Department of Navy (DON) networks. The work addressed the following question: What security tool components are required for effective deployment on afloat platforms and at ashore support organizations for the execution of DCO workflows and playbooks?

As part of Phase III, Stage 1, my thesis established the workflows and playbooks to be used during the analysis and evaluation of CWS Phase III, Stage 2, where virtual experimentation will occur in the Persistent Cyber Training Environment (PCTE). CWS Phase III, Stage 2 will emulate the ashore support team's augmentation of local cyber defense capabilities by injecting advanced analytics and programmatic courses of action via the workflows and playbooks. The objective of CWS Phase III, Stage 2 is to determine how automated playbooks, in parallel with federated SOAR and SIEM toolsets, can augment afloat cyber defense in a disconnected and intermittent bandwidth environment.

A challenge to virtual testing was to identify the correct environment in Phase III, Stage 1 to host the experiment at a later date within Stage 2. The environment must simulate a real-world network on a DON platform. The PCTE provides an environment comparable to a DON platform. Splunk SOAR and the Elasticsearch, Logstash, and Kibana (ELK) Stack SIEM are the systems that will be used in the simulated environment. In Phase III, Stage 2, three automated playbooks will be executed within the environment hosting federated SIEM and SOAR solutions to challenge IR methods, architecture configurations, and cyber defense of the emulated afloat platform in a disconnected and intermittent network.

The first aim of my thesis was to establish two partitioned architectures within PCTE. The first partition established was the afloat environment, which will simulate a Littoral Combat Ship (LCS), and its associated network topology, Consolidated Afloat Networks, and Enterprise Services (CANES). This environment currently resides in PCTE and is comprised of several virtual machines including a DNS server, proxy server, domain controller, mail server, host-based rogue sensor, file server, application server, and intrusion detection manager. These virtual machines were equipped with EDR agents to monitor and collect data fed to the afloat SIEM. The SIEM acquires information from each of the endpoint EDR agents, then aggregates and federates this information to the SIEM ashore. The second partition of the PCTE environment is the ashore support environment. In this environment, the ashore SIEM receives an aggregated feed from the afloat SIEM and then provides that information to the ashore SOAR. The ashore SOAR is connected to the internet and receives valuable threat enrichment information, which the ashore operator can use to determine which remediation playbook to send to the afloat

SOAR. The architecture will be implemented in CWS Phase III, Stage 2.

The second aim of my thesis was to select IR workflows and playbooks for vendor development. Workflows are logical codifications of procedures that allow for automation, and playbooks are a set of rules that define one or more courses of action triggered by one or multiple events. During a Tabletop Exercise (TTX), in December 2021, organized by this capstone, stakeholders identified a notional workflow for automated remediation tasks, which require the orchestration of tasks to be conducted through the cooperation of the shipboard defenders and the ashore experts. Stakeholders then developed a matrix to decide how to categorize cyber incidents and selected three incidents to be tested during CWS Phase III, Stage 2. Navy Cyber Defense Operations Command (NCDOC) had provided the ten most frequently detected and reported fleet cyber incidents in the last five years. The objective is to use these to test playbooks for remediation in the PCTE. During CWS Phase III, Stage 1 cyber incident responses were qualitatively categorized into harmless, reversible, and irreversible playbooks. Next, three of these playbooks were selected to be built by the CWS SOAR vendors. Each playbook will include a course of action for each cyber incident injected.

The CWS Phase III, Stage 2 objective is to observe the experiments and analyze whether the playbooks developed by CWS vendors during Phase III, Stage 1 meet requirements determined by the Navy. Testing the SOAR/SIEM technologies with workflows and playbooks representative of actual DON incidents can help the CWS contribute to improvement in the way afloat and ashore defenders interact, support, and defend afloat networks.

It was a lot of work and long hours of writing, proofreading, and reviews by professors. Then it was kicked back to me so I could make corrections, but I was able to graduate in March of 2022 and I was assigned orders to US Fleet Cyber Command/ US Tenth Fleet (FCC/C10F) in Fort Meade, Maryland, which was my final Navy command since I will retire in 2025.

CHAPTER XIII

I had to drive to the East Coast, so that was another cross-country trip. I planned to stop in as many cities where I could watch a baseball game as I could. Baseball is the most popular sport in Dominican Republic, and I grew up enjoying the sport. Soccer, or futbol, had taken the number-one spot in my heart, but I still enjoyed baseball a lot, so I decided that this trip would be an amazing opportunity to see as many stadiums as possible. I started my journey out of Monterey, California, then my first stop was Salt Lake City, Utah. No baseball here, but I needed a good stopping point and some good food. Next, it was Denver and there I spent the evening having dinner with my cousin and his wife, who lived there, and then the next day, I watched the Colorado Rockies in their beautiful stadium. Kansas City was next; the weather was beautiful since it was April of 2022. I watched the Kansas City Royals and enjoyed some awesome BBQ.

From there, I drove to Minneapolis and watched the Minnesota Twins; their stadium was one of the most beautiful places on the trip. I drove a few miles to Milwaukee and met my boy and his wife for an afternoon of conversation and laughs before I watched the Milwaukee Brewers. Then I went back down to St. Louis so I could watch the Cardinals. I tried to watch a game each day, which is why I had to do a few up and downs through the country, because the games didn't match with my driving schedule. Lastly, I stopped in Chicago for a few days and had a blast with Emily. We had amazing food and watched the Chicago Cubs at the famous Wrigley Field. After that, it was time to visit Indianapolis and see another friend, who I had dinner with. I had not seen her in years, so it was really good to catch up. I wanted to see a game in Cincinnati, but the Reds had an away series, so no games in the ballpark. By now, I was exhausted from driving so I decided to drive to my final destination. I made it to Maryland in early May of 2022.

Only a few weeks after reporting to my new command, I was given the news that I was promoted to the rank of Master Chief Petty Officer. It had taken over seven years to get selected, so I was a bit shocked and emotional. I spoke with my Command Master Chief, or CMC; he said that he was impressed with me staying Navy after what I endured with the bombing of the USS *Cole*. He asked if it was ok if we did an article about me and dealing with mental health since it was such a big topic in the Navy and society. He also introduced me to the Navy initiative about resilience, warrior toughness. Warrior toughness (WT) was a holistic human performance skillset that enhanced the toughness of our Sailors with a focus on the pursuit of peak performance. The system emphasized coequal development of toughness in the mind, body, and soul. WT combines performance psychology skills with character development, and taught the warrior mindset. WT trained Sailors to approach tasks utilizing the warrior mindset, which is a high-performance model that emphasized a cycle of commitment, preparation, execution, and reflection. When completed repeatedly, this continuum built and sustained toughness while progressing toward peak performance.

Lastly, in warrior toughness Sailors were taught performance psychology skills. Through applied skills training, Sailors were provided empirically based mindfulness and performance psychology techniques proven to enhance the ability to perform at peak capacity. The skills taught were: recalibrate, mindfulness, goal setting, self-talk, mental rehearsal, and energy management. My CMC said that I should go to the commands around the world and teach the class to each of our Sailors. He said I would be a great example as the warrior and show Sailors that we can achieve great things by being resilient.

I waited until I could go to the school for warrior toughness since I couldn't go until after October of 2022. CMC spoke with our Public Affairs Office so they could do a story about me going from E-1 to E-9 while struggling with PTSD and mental health, and how I was able to keep my security clearance even though I was seeing a psychiatrist. The article was very well done, and it was published in June of 2022 by our command media team. It was called "Undefeated, This Flag Will Fly: Seaman Tackled PTSD to Make Master Chief." The article was a hit as it was published on many Navy-related websites and even in the *All Hands* magazine. Because of that, I was asked to talk at many events. One of the first events I spoke at was at the Naval Academy in Annapolis. I had to speak to the plebes, which was the summer training program that was required of all incoming freshmen to the United States Naval Academy.

The program lasted approximately seven weeks and consisted of rigorous physical and mental training. The stated purpose of Plebe Summer, according to the Academy, is to turn civilians into midshipmen.

There were about 1,200 plebes inside the auditorium, and I had an hour to speak about my experience onboard the *Cole* from the damage control perspective and then also answer questions. I was nervous at first, but as I started to talk about my recollection of the events, I was able to have tunnel vision until it was time to ask questions. I was happily surprised how much they took in from the amount and quality of questions. I had to stop taking questions because my time was up and the next speaker was due to speak. It was a very humbling experience, but it gave me the courage to do it again in different venues and settings.

August of 2022 comes, and now it was time to help E-6 transition to E-7 by going through the Chief season. As a Master Chief, it was my responsibility to train and prepare our Chiefs because they were my relief and the ones that would continue to take care of our Sailors and carry on the customs and traditions. I was asked to travel to Fort Worth, Texas, and speak with a group of twenty selected Chiefs and a command of 200-plus Sailors. It was another session where the questions were very relevant to the conversation and events I was describing about the *Cole* and my life. Then I received an invitation to be the guest speaker for the khaki ball after the Chief season was completed. I traveled to Colorado Springs, Northern Virginia, and the khaki ball for my region, so I got to speak to the new and current Chiefs of my area. Here is the speech I wrote and the one I will keep using, with minor changes:

"I want to say thank you for the opportunity to be the speaker today. It is truly a humbling experience, an honor, and I hope you can all take something positive from my 3 key points."

Being the Chief. You're now the SME!! You're required to put your Sailors FIRST, since you don't get to work until they go home. You're the chief 24/7/365, your conduct is judged each second and with each decision. You now have anchors on your collar and with it you're giving a privilege no other senior enlisted is giving, the trust and backing of 130 years of proud history. You were pinned _____ but because of the history of those anchors, you could have walked to your CO's office on the next day and said "Sir/Ma'am this is how we will accomplish this mission, take care of these Sailors or fix this equipment" and he or she will trust you because you and the CO understand the responsibility we inherited as Chiefs. As the Chief, you have to lead our Sailors though the good, bad, and sometimes very ugly, because you're now the CHIEF!

Humbleness. It's humble to ask for help from the mess and your Sailors (we don't know it all, even about our rates or programs that we might have been in charge of for years), humble to have mentors of different backgrounds (this includes gender, race, pay grade, and rating); your perspective will only be more prosperous by the diversity you surround yourself with. Humble to be corrected by our brothers and sisters and humble to lean on the mess for guidance and support, because if you look bad, then the entire Chiefs' Mess looks bad. Finally, be humble, to be honest with yourself about your shortcomings and what you need to work on, so you can be a better person, leader, and sailor.

Legacy. What's your legacy? (close your eyes for a second and I want you to think about a sailor that has motivated you, who has pushed you, someone that was there when you lost hope or just needed help . . . Do you remember what ribbons they had? Do you remember what enlisted warfare pin they had? I bet you don't). Because your legacy is not what ribbons or warfare device you have or how many EP evals you have received through the years. Your legacy is how you treat people, how you push them to be the best person they can be, how you help them day in and day out. Your legacy is that sea story being told today or tomorrow about you that starts with 'my Chief did this.' That said, your legacy to others will not always be favorable. Sometimes it is because of the mistakes we made as we were learning how to lead. If this is the case, then I hope that you learn from it and continue to get better. Other times, it is simply because you're holding them accountable. In this case, I will just say if you demand less, you will get less. Your personal legacy is not just the uniform or the anchors we wear. Here in this amazing group with have individuals that have PhDs, Masters, Bachelors, certifications, do volunteer work, own businesses, completed marathons, climbed the highest peaks, are amazing parents, daughters and sons, etc. So my point is be sure to work on your personal legacy as well because we will all move on from the military, and I will hate for any of you to lose your own identity once you can't wear the uniform anymore.

In conclusion, thank you for making me look back at my fourteen years wearing anchors and think about the good and the bad that got me here and for FY-XXX class . . . BE YOU, BE GREAT, BE ACCOUNTABLE!!"

I received a lot of compliments and positive feedback on the speech at each location, and how they related or saw what I was trying to convey. I even had some that told me how much it motivated them to continue to be the best Chief they could be and to see how they made an impact daily. It felt really good to hear that from my peers since my only desire was to touch at least one person at each event.

In September of 2022, I was walking to another office, and in the hallway I saw this beautiful lady and I smiled at her. She kind of smiled but nothing too crazy, so I didn't want to disturb her and kept walking. Facebook suggested her as a friend a few days later, so I messaged her and just simply asked if she was still in town. She said she was about to take off or already on the flight. We talked for a bit, and then I told her to let me know when she landed so I knew she was ok. We continued to talk and made arrangements for me to go visit her across the country. We both had a lot going on but we decided on a weekend to meet, and we had an amazing time together. I met some of her friends and learned more about her. We continued to see each other at every opportunity. We both loved to travel and have adventures, so it was easy to plan things and go to different places to explore and find yummy food.

I was looking forward to this month, November of 2022, because I was going to do another trip with my daughter. This time it was extra special because I shared with her one of my bucket list trips: A trip to see the World Cup!! I wanted to see Lionel Messi since I was certain that would be his last World Cup. I also wanted to see another country with my daughter, and Qatar offered luxury but also another perspective on how others lived life. We spent five days there and watched three matches. We explored the city, which was upgraded with more luxury, public transportation, and just a bigger infrastructure to accommodate the influx of tourists. My daughter was surprised to see how the locals looked at her tattoos and shorts, or tops with no sleeves; to them she was showing too much skin. This was even more ironic when you thought of the fact that you had over two million people from all over the world and with different views on things, yet the locals still had a hard time with women wearing certain things.

We even ran into one of my cousins and his wife; just another blessing that I was able to share with my princess. Since I wanted to ensure we got to see Lionel Messi, we only watched group stage matches. Once we returned, I continued to watch the matches and my lady came to see me before the holidays. We watched the World Cup final together, even if she never really watched soccer before. Thankfully, Argentina made it to the final and they played the previous champion, France. We had a blast cooking and had snacks ready, and we just enjoyed what I will say was the greatest World Cup final. I noticed that I had no desire to spend the holidays with anybody since I couldn't spend it with my children. I realized that it was the norm for years. I just stayed on my own or went to work because I didn't have anywhere to go or didn't feel like talking to anybody. I set some goals for myself for the New Year. I just wanted to be very focused and intentional. I wanted to start pouring more into my children, friendships, and my Sailors.

My first goal was to get into the class for warrior toughness. I wanted to sit in on the class my command was teaching and then go to the actual class that awarded the NEC for the class, which meant that I was able to give the training to my command. So, in January of 2023, I attended the class that I would be taking over once I received the NEC. It was easy to see how much this could benefit our Sailors if done with purpose and with the intention to help people. The instructors were my Command Master Chief, a chaplain, and a resiliency officer. Each of them had attended the NEC course and were more knowledgeable of what the Navy was trying to achieve.

It was February of 2023, and I went to school to become Advanced Warrior Toughness (AWT) certified. That way, I'd be able to teach the curriculum together with a chaplain and a resiliency counselor. The class was five days long, and it was a nice mixture of different ranks and Navy communities. This brought out a lot of perspectives and different views. Once I graduated, I partnered up with the rest of the team to see the material we were using to teach and ensure I was prepared to do my part of the presentation.

I didn't know when I embarked in the journey of teaching the class that I would get so much from it. I had this amazing desire to inspire others, help others see the best version of themselves, and motivate others to push forward while giving themselves grace. The class was going to be done in three days. The first day, I talked about the warrior mentality and the chaplain spoke about the soul. The soul in the sense of finding out why, what drives you when things are dark, or when you want to achieve the impossible. Then I taught them about the importance of telling a relevant sea story and how that helped unite us in the Navy. The second day, the resilience counselor taught the class about the different performance techniques to help the body be in tune with the mind and soul. The third day was about hearing their own sea stories that emphasized a cycle of commitment, preparation, execution, and reflection. They also performed teach-backs on the different performance techniques. In those three days, we shared experiences, views, opinions, and perspectives.

Our first trip was to Bahrain, where we had a great mix of pay grades and beliefs. The people that had been in the Navy for over ten years believed that they didn't have to be taught anything about toughness, since they had seen and done it all. The ones under ten years didn't believe that they were warriors or didn't want to be called warriors because they worked in front of computers or they worked on equipment that was local without any impact downrange. Understanding the purpose of the program, I conveyed that there was a different way to look at the program if they felt like warrior or toughness didn't identify who they were. The program was about peak performance, about an individual being able to handle adversity, and become the best version of themselves. It was to make each student realize that we would never be at 100 percent, but that they could give 100 percent of what they had. So, for example, today I might feel like all I have to give at work or at home is 50 percent of me. Then the warrior toughness techniques will help me give the full 50 percent while giving me tools to, hopefully, make tomorrow a 51 percent day. It was interesting to see how vulnerable a lot of those Sailors were, how the Navy was just a mirror of society, and the suicide rate and mental health issues that plague society are part of the Navy as well.

After Bahrain, we headed to Japan in May of 2023. I was extremely excited since it was my first time going to Japan. We landed on Saturday morning, so I explored Tokyo all Sunday since the class didn't start until Tuesday. Tokyo was so clean, easy to get around, and with lots of options for food and shopping. This class was a bit different since most of them were twenty-two or younger and in their first Navy command, plus away from home in a foreign country. During the times we shared perspectives and experiences, you could hear the negativity and distrust for leadership and Navy as a whole. Then, during the sea story time, they shared some really intimate experiences and feelings. Two of the participants tried to commit suicide before the age of twenty-one; another three were dealing with depression and anxiety. It was sad to see and hear so much pain at that early stage of these young adults lives, but I was also grateful that they felt comfortable enough to share those things with us. It also made them become closer with each other since they understood one another better. The team left Japan with a new sense of purpose. We understood more than ever how much talking about resiliency and how to cope with life's challenges benefited our Sailors. A couple of weeks after Japan, we made trips to Suffolk, Virginia and Pensacola, Florida. These were more opportunities to engage with Sailors and teach those techniques that would help them be the best person they could be.

By August of 2023, I had visited seven different commands under the umbrella of my current command, spoke with over 200 Sailors, and taught many of the techniques hundreds of times. I'm focused on giving all I have for my Sailors while also preparing myself for the next chapter of my life, retirement from the Navy. The Navy is all I've known for the past twenty-four years, and by the time I retire in 2025, it will be twenty-six years of being a sailor. So I have to make sure my resume is up to par so I can get a decent job. I have to go to medical and get everything checked out so I have a way ahead for any issues discovered from my duties in the last twenty-six years. Lastly, I think about where I want to settle down for good. What do I want to do with my life? Work as an IT? Cyber security manager? Do public speaking? Own a business? The options are truly endless if I prepare myself.

Years passed. The commands, port visits, and even women came and went, and my children's lives sped by. There was a time when I did not know what my life would become, a time when I could not see past the streets of Union City, Jersey. Then the Navy happened, and with it my life changed forever. Through it all, a few constants remained. My loving mother, who stuck with me even when I did not have any love for her. My desire to be the best at all I do and to make others better. Then, lastly, my children, who picked me up when I was in the darkest place, both in my mind and heart. All that brought me here.

So I decided to put all my memories and events on paper because I want my children to know more about me. Because I'm hoping to inspire a young man or woman who is going through a difficult time or just don't see themselves achieving the impossible, and because I want to thank all the people that have had an influence on me.

My childhood was not ideal, and I have a lot of trauma because of it, but it really defines who I am. My love for my children is because I desperately wanted to feel loved and at many times I didn't get that, so I never want my children to not feel my love and devotion to them. I owe my childhood my love languages. I am a physical touch and words of affirmation person because, again, I needed those things badly but, unfortunately, I was not getting them. I'm grateful that I'm this way now. I'm able to be as loving as possible to those I care about and able to understand that saying thank you, telling someone that they're doing great, or that they make you feel special is always a beautiful thing in my eyes.

The time in the Navy is another history. It's how I became a man in many aspects. I was part of a tragedy early in my career, and that had its own traumatic effect as well as lasting effects on how I behaved and developed through the years. Seeing so much death at nineteen years old is something that I don't wish on anybody, and it's something that will always be part of me because my PTSD will always be there. I have learned to live with it, and, most importantly, I have had many people who have shown me love and care. Their desire to see me do well and show me love is truly amazing. I would be remiss if I didn't talk about the amazing things the Navy has afforded me. My children and I have a better life due to the opportunities in the Navy. I have two master's degrees, without any debt thanks to the Navy; I have seen fifty-plus countries and ninety-plus cities across the world thanks to the Navy. Then you add the incredible people I have met, the amazing people who have become friends and the very lucky few who I consider family; it all has been a blessing. A blessing because I'm richer emotionally, physically, and mentally because of them.

To all the women that I hurt, used, cared for, loved, and even made hate me, I apologize. I apologize for only caring about what I wanted and cared for. I apologize for not worrying about your feelings, and for making you unhappy, for making you feel less than, that you had flaws or that you were not good enough because of the things I did to you or that you had to discover later on. I apologize for not maturing and being honest until my late thirties, and I apologize for ever making you cry.

To my mother, I hope that I made you proud. That all the sacrifices you made for me and my brother were not in vain, that you only having two pairs of jeans was not a sacrifice you did for nothing. You had a tough childhood and life, so the least I could do is to give you a son that you can be proud of, a son that adores you and a son that forever will be a mama's boy! I don't have a lot to say about my father. I love him and I will never wish him harm, but I don't believe he was a great father to me. I learned to never lie to your children because of him. I wish that lesson would have been learned by conversation, not because I had experienced it as a child from my dad.

To all the Sailors who I have worked for, worked with, or who have worked for me, thank you! Thank you for teaching me how to be compassionate, resilient, and determined, for encouraging me to be better, to never be satisfied, and to take every opportunity given to me and give it 100 percent. Each sailor has given me a different perspective in life, on how to follow and how to lead. To understand that race, ethnicity, gender, religion, sexuality, and economic status doesn't matter when you understand we're all the same. That each of us just want to do the very best and make someone we love proud and even provide a better life. I was extremely homophobic and just rude to anybody that was different. Thanks to the Sailors I had the pleasure to serve with, I'm a person that embraces everyone and wants to make everyone smile.

My children, my heart is full each day because of you. Since my princess was born and then double once my prince was born, my children have been my why. My why to keep pushing forward, my why to not give up without a fight, my why to be a better person than yesterday. Seeing each of you grow and become your own person is my pure joy. I'm so grateful and lucky to be your dad, to be loved by each of you, and have the privilege to teach you and help you navigate this crazy and unpredictable world. I want to always be the love that I was not able to receive!

To my future wife, your support and love has been unparalleled and unexpected. I was caught by your physical beauty and presence, but it is truly your heart and mind that made me love you. I'm lucky to be around you, share a meaningful conversation, and make plans about our future. You're my calm, my positive perspective, and the reason why I'm writing my thoughts down.

To anybody that has decided to embark with me on this journey, thank you. I hope you smiled, learned a bit about the Navy, and feel like you can accomplish anything, because an average person like me has been capable of accomplishing so much. We all have so much to offer if we really set our mind to it. I wish I could tell you how to tap into your best self, but we all have different triggers. We all have a different why, but I will only say that it is urgent that you get ahold of your "why." Having something that you can look to as a light to be better, to be more, to be the best version of you . . . is incredibly powerful. I was not aware that I had a why early on in my life, but just as we mature, my why has evolved from my mother, to my children, to just wanting to live my life to the fullest. If you take anything from my words, take that much; the importance of having a why, the importance to give yourself grace, and the importance of being a kind person to those around you.

Made in the USA
Middletown, DE
07 September 2024

60523121R00115